QUANTUM PHYSICS

FOR BEGINNERS

A COMPLETE GUIDE TO ITS MAIN PRINCIPLES, THEORIES,
AND MYSTERIES. DISCOVER HOW QUANTUM PHYSICS
HELPS US IMPROVE THE RELATIONSHIP WITH
OURSELVES AND OUR PLANET

SUSANNE DAM NYGAARD

Imagination is more important than knowledge. Knowledge is limited, imagination embraces the world, stimulating progress, giving birth to evolution.

Albert Einstein (1929)

TABLE OF CONTENTS

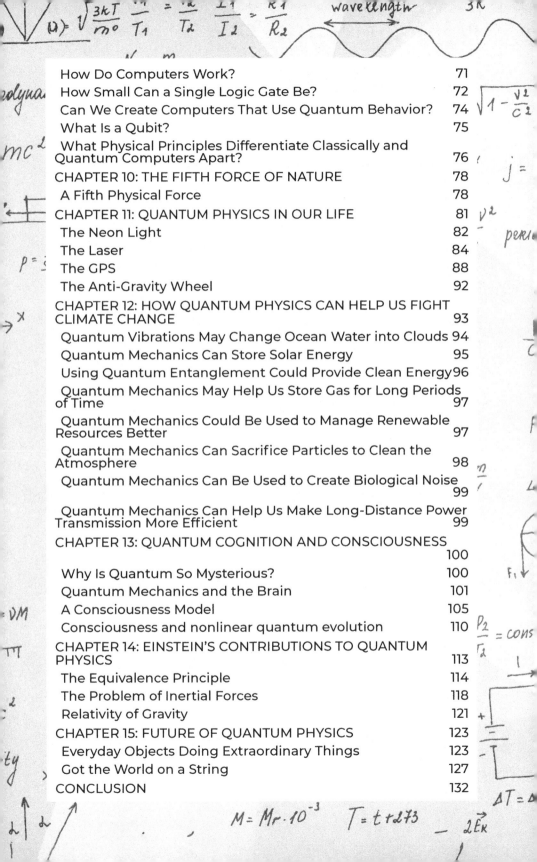

INTRODUCTION

Before we go forward to examine what quantum physics is, we must first have an understanding of the two distinct words that make up the term: quantum and physics. Physics is derived from the Greek word *physika*, which could be said to mean "observable." It is an arm or area of science that has to do with matter structure, movement, and behavior across time and space.

Physics also seeks to explain the relationship between fundamental components of the universe, such as forces and energy (at least, the part that is observable). As a natural science, it deals with every part of nature, which includes both microscopic and submicroscopic constituents. Simply put, physics seeks to explain why the universe behaves as it does.

On the other hand, *quantum* is the term used to describe the part of the universe that is super small or subatomic. It has a Latin meaning of "how much." It deals with how many units of energy and data can be predicted and observed in the field of quantum physics. Quantum deals with a strange and ghostly matter that defiles the rules and patterns of behavior of visible matter.

In a quantum state, matter exists, and at the same time, it does not exist. This is the reason several scientists have been able to predict where they might be but haven't really been able to know where they actually are. The quantum world includes photons (particles that form light and radiation), electrons, protons, etc.

The branch of physics that can explain how these ghostly matters, or how the universe's smallest constituents, behave is known as quantum physics. This branch of physics was first attributed to the work of Max Planck when he wrote a book on blackbody radiation. This field was then developed by Niels Bohr, Werner Heisenberg, Richard Feynman, Erwin Schrodinger, and Albert Einstein. Although, it must be said that Albert Einstein's goal was to modify or even to disprove this branch of physics because he had a theoretical issue with it.

So then, what is quantum physics?

Quantum physics is the subdivision of physics dealing with the study of matter and energy at their smallest or most fundamental form. This means that quantum physics studies matter and energy either at the atomic, molecular, smaller microscopic, or nuclear levels. Quantum physics is needed to fully understand the structure and atomic composition of matter.

The atom is the smallest unit of an element, and a group of atoms forms molecules, which are the smallest unit of a compound. For example, water molecules in a stream, even though they cannot be seen, are definitely present. In studying energies, quantum physics divides energies into packets that are indivisible. These packets are known as quanta.

Quanta is a discrete or minimum unit or quantity of energy that is proportional in magnitude to the radiation it produces during an interaction. Around the early 20th century, scientists came to realize that the customary laws that guided macroscopic matters could not be applied to more minor microscopic matter. This is because these microscopic objects or particles (as they are often referred to) have their own unique behavior. They could either or at the same time behave as particles or objects and also act as waves. A clear example of an object that behaves like this is the photon.

Photon is an example of a fundamental particle, and it is the quantum of electromagnetic radiation, which includes radio and light waves. Note, photons do not have mass and are packets of energy. The behavior of light has raised many controversies. First, it was believed that light behaved as particle streams of bright balls. But later, after some experiments, it was believed that light traveled as waves.

Now, much more recently, the belief is that light can both act as particles and waves, which are now referred to as photons. There are groups of scientists who are still divided on the nature of photons, either particle or wave, while others meet at the middle describing the behavior of photons as "wavicle." According to this group of scientists, the nature to ascribe to how light travels is dependent on the scientist's individual measurement of a photon.

Note, a photon can only be measured as either wave or particles, but it cannot be both at the same time. This mystery or difficulty in measurement is not unique to photons alone, but it is also common in measuring protons, electrons, and every atom that either exists in the quantum state or has been quantized.

When objects are quantized, they lose continuity because they can only be recorded to exist in a restricted quantity or a particular state at a time. In fact, all fundamental particles or objects possess the properties of either being measured as waves or particles. This dilemma is the origin of the idea or theory of wave-particle duality, which is the major focus of quantum physics.

Quantum physics explains how and why biology and chemistry function or work the way they do. It is believed that it influences the behavior of atoms, and as such, it influences every other element. Quantum physics is the only branch of physics that can explain the *hows* that other branches cannot, for example, the way electrons travel through the computer and the mechanism behind the burning of the sun. It also explains how photons through the solar panel are transformed into electrical currents or, in other cases, turned into laser beams.

Similar to the other branch of physics known as classical physics, quantum physics is also divided into subfields. These subfields are quantum optics, electrodynamics, gravity, and mechanics. Although quantum physics has a broader scope and encompasses every other subfield, it is often used interchangeably with quantum field or quantum mechanics. While visible classical physics is used to explain large and slow-moving objects, quantum mechanics is used to explain nonvisible (at least to the natural eyes) and very fast-moving objects. So, put simply, quantum mechanics can be the same as classical physics when dealing with objects that fall under the first category.

CHAPTER 1: LET ME EXPLAIN WHAT QUANTUM PHYSICS IS

Scientific advancements seem to happen every day, and quantum mechanics is no exception. Although the discipline is relatively new, many people are familiar with it because of major discoveries that have made their way into popular culture. For example, Albert Einstein's theory of general relativity has influenced movies such as "Interstellar" and "The Theory of Everything".

Quantum physics is an advanced branch of physics that includes subatomic particles like photons and electrons. Many people have heard of these particles and even these concepts, but many do not understand how quantum physics is different from other fields in physics. The following will discuss some major differences between quantum mechanics and classical physics.

These are some of the most important differences:

Classical physics does not include the uncertainty principle. This means a set of determined values for certain properties for each object (such as position, velocity, and momentum). However, according to quantum mechanics, certain properties are considered "uncertain" because they can be either a value or within a certain range depending on what situation is observed. The uncertainty principle involves the Heisenberg's uncertainty relations. These relations state that it is impossible to know the exact position and momentum of a particle simultaneously, or the exact position and time of a particle at the same time.

This means that quantum mechanics does not predict things with absolute certainty like classical physics. Instead, quantum mechanics predicts various probabilities for certain outcomes, called "wave functions". The wave functions are obtained from a mathematical model based on Schrödinger's equation. This equation describes narrow regions where particles can be found in nature and determines possible results of measurements on these particles.

This always leads to a probability that contains a quantum number, a base 2 logarithm of the ratio of observed results/total results. The most important rule in this is the Born rule, which states that the probability of an outcome can be found by taking the square root of a complex number.

It is important to consider what trying to determine something with 100% certainty means when looking into this topic further. It would not be possible to witness something unless it is viewed by someone (i.e., humans). But since humans are not perfectly accurate observers, they could never detect anything with 100% certainty (nor could they due to limitations on their abilities in other fields). If quantum mechanics were limited to the human view, it would not be useful. In a way, what is lacking from classical physics is that we can never know for sure what particles look like and the other subatomic particles and forces.

In classical physics when you experiment you always have a book in which you write down the results and observations (i.e., if you measure objects' volume then this is recorded in the book). However, in quantum mechanics these results are listed in probability distributions. This means that each observation could be found somewhere between a certain range of values (in terms of probabilities).

Getting Familiar with Quantum Physics

Now that you know the basics of quantum mechanics and how it differs from classical physics, you may be interested in looking into it further. There are many aspects of quantum mechanics that can help improve our understanding of the world, but there are also many challenges to consider.

The following will talk about challenges in quantum mechanics and attempts to overcome them:

Quantum computers have changed the way we look at computation and computation power. Quantum computers use quantum information to perform calculations with higher speeds than what is provided by classical computers. Since they are based on quantum mechanics, they can give much faster results than ordinary computers (which run on classical physics). This is mostly due to the nature of quantum mechanics, which allows faster calculations to be performed using parallelism.

Quantum computers can surpass other forms of computation in many ways, but various challenges need to be overcome for this technology to become a reality. To start, the main challenge is how fragile quantum computers are when it comes to their environment. Quantum computers rely on individual particles and small systems to work properly. However, since these particles are so delicate, they can be disrupted by noise surrounding them (which also happens due to heat). Since most particles cannot be observed without changing what they represent, it is challenging for scientists and engineers to keep them intact while being observed and manipulated.

Another challenge encountered when dealing with quantum computers is the communication between particles. Any two particles to communicate with each other requires either energy to be transferred between the particles or weak magnetic forces to interact. For these forces to happen, more surface area must be provided for them to interact. This limits how small a system can be and how much it can do (since small systems do not have as much room to move around).

Einstein's theory of special relativity has some major flaws and weaknesses that need to corrected by theorists. The major flaw involves faster-than-light travel, which has been disproven by experiments involving the neutrino. The neutrino was observed through signaling from the CERN near Geneva, Switzerland to Gran Sasso Laboratory in Italy. It was sent in a beam that was supposed to travel faster than the speed of light, but due to the technology of detecting signals in both locations it cannot be confirmed if this happened or not. This means that there are problems with special relativity theory. However, scientists are still trying to use it as a sort of "analogy" since it is so correct to observe things (it is believed to become more accurate as they understand quantum mechanics more).

Another major problem with special relativity is that it cannot properly explain how gravity works at extremely large scales. These large scales are as small as a galaxy, but still billions and billions of times larger than the atomic scale. The issue lies in that gravity can cause atoms to become "frozen" and not continue to move. This corresponds to what is known about the gravitational force of a black hole, which can cause mass to be "devoured".

Another problem with special relativity is that it does not allow time travel. According to special relativity, time cannot be traveled faster than light (since this would violate causality). Although one can argue that processes can occur in the universe but not be observed (such as the Big Bang), there is no way to travel back in time using special relativity.

Another problem with classical physics is that it does not allow infinite speeds or energy to be achieved. This is due to relativity, which states that anything traveling at a certain speed will produce mass. If infinite speed were achieved, the mass would increase infinitely until sufficient energy could no longer be provided. This means that if one wanted to travel at an infinite speed, they would need an infinite amount of energy to escape gravitational forces (which keep objects on earth).

Quantum Mechanics Is Discrete

One of the biggest problems with classical physics theories is inherent weaknesses and flaws within these theories. Conventional physics does not allow for a complete understanding of the universe, so theories such as gravity cannot be fully understood. In addition, classical physics does not provide a good explanation for how this universe began, what happened in the Big Bang or even why humans exist. However, many areas within quantum mechanics have yet to be explained and added to our knowledge domain (such as quantum gravity).

Quantum mechanics has several advantages over classical physics. Those who do not understand this will favor quantum mechanics and become more skeptical of its drawbacks (despite it being harder to prove). The most obvious advantage is that quantum mechanics can generate particles in an infinite number of parallel universes, which results in a much faster computation speed. This means that quantum computers can process large values and achieve much faster results than classical computers.

Quantum mechanics also allows for correlation between multiple particles without having a single "ensemble" (for example one particle acting like another). This allows for more information to be shared among the particles and it is not as limiting as classical physics because it does not need to be limited to a subset of particles.

Quantum Physics Involves Probability

Even though quantum mechanics is a very complicated topic, it is also very relevant to the living world. One of the main problems with classical physics can be directly tied to probabilities. The most major problem with classical physics is that it does not include or adequately explain probability or randomness. Instead, classical physics assumes that everything happens based on cause and effect. This means that for something to happen there needs to be a starting point, which means that every particle must start at a certain point and every event must exist before another one (which requires more than being in motion). However, this logic does not apply when dealing with many things simultaneously, which is how biological cells work (they use probability to operate).

Another major problem recognized within classical physics is that it does not explain black holes and does not provide an adequate explanation for the Big Bang. In addition, classical physics cannot explain why all objects carry an inherent momentum. Accordingly, these issues are all factors in how our universe works and what we observe today. But since these are "fundamental" problems with classical physics when dealing with the living world, scientists should take advantage of quantum mechanics to better understand the universe.

Quantum Physics Is a Nonlocal Science

A major problem with quantum mechanics is that it is not directly visible to us. This means that many people will ignore the problems with classical physics and view quantum mechanics as "just a theory". In addition, when scientists use the double slit experiment to prove that matter behaves like waves, they expect observers to believe them. Scientists explain that this is impossible by saying that if the double slit experiment were done by one person (A), everyone else would see different results because of their perspective. But what scientists fail to consider is that this problem exists because we do not have a good model for observing quantum properties.

Science has shown us what is possible in the world (by combining quantum mechanics with relativity and laws of thermodynamics). But our knowledge of reality has not shown us what is truly "unbroken" or nonlocal. For example, a person's brain can operate like a computer (even though it is nonlocal). This means that people observe the same events but their experiences will be different due to how their brains operate. Quantum physics does not properly explain this problem and even suggests that two observers viewing the same event may result in completely different observations. Therefore, science cannot adequately explain how our universe works without quantum mechanics providing a better understanding.

Quantum Mechanics Is Responsible for The Atomic Theory

Nuclear physics and chemistry have made more progress in the last 30 years than in the previous 300. However, this increase in knowledge can be directly linked to quantum mechanics. Many people will agree that nuclear physics could not progress without quantum mechanics. Nuclear physics has never explained the atomic theory (the ability to form atoms from a simple nucleus). The big bang starts the universe with a "singularity" (a point where all matter and energy combined). This theory is not proven because of how scientists view space as having time. There should have been a single point at which time and space started forming, but there is no solid evidence for it.

Quantum mechanics can describe the interactions between quarks, electrons and photons to form atoms. In addition, quantum mechanics can also describe the dynamic nature of atomic nuclei and demonstrate how protons interact to form a nucleus. Quantum mechanics does not attempt to disprove the atomic theory, but it provides better explanations for why atoms form in our universe.

Quantum Physics Is Quite Small

Quantum mechanics can be applied to as small as a few subatomic particles. However, there are new problems when dealing with smaller particles because the number of particles is limited and humans do not have a good way to observe them. Our best tools for observing quantum properties are microscopic devices called "microscopes" which have been around for over 400 years. At first microscopes helped scientists figure out what light was made of, but it did not provide a good solution to observing small objects because light is still a wave (which means it cannot show us what we need to see).

Quantum mechanics has developed a new way for us to see the subatomic world, which involves observing electrons. Electrons can be perceived within a microscope without looking through light. In addition, there is no doubt that by using quantum mechanics we have found new forms of matter.

Quantum Physics Can Explain Time Travel

The key feature of quantum mechanics is that it can apply to both small and large objects as they interact with each other. This allows scientists to predict how a large object will react when interacting with a small one (and vice versa). In addition, quantum mechanics has application to time travel. This is referred to as the "quantum paradox" and would mean that something could change the past and affect the future. We have no way of understanding how this occurs, which means that it is just something scientists need to accept.

Many physicists will ignore this problem because they do not understand it or have never encountered it within their studies. They see all their work as valid and only consider results consistent with their theories (which would not include time travel).

But what scientists do not realize is that time travel may exist in our world because of quantum mechanics (and other unknown phenomena). However, all science does is explain what we observe today and what we can currently measure.

Quantum Physics Isn't Wizardry

Many people will reject quantum mechanics because they view it as a "wizard's tool". The fact that quantum mechanics works in our universe does not mean that it was created to solve problems. The ability to predict small interactions demonstrates the power of quantum mechanics (and how it can extend our understanding of the universe).

Many scientists will do everything they can to disprove the acceptance of quantum mechanics and even consider it impossible. This is because they were never taught about it at school and they are simply following a set of laws based on their observations.

On top of this, many scientists do not understand how subatomic particles interact. This is because humans cannot directly observe these interactions and we have only been able to quantify them with mathematical equations. But this does not mean that quantum mechanical laws are invalid. The mathematics of these equations is correct and the results are consistent with quantum theory.

CHAPTER 2: QUANTUM THEORY: WHAT YOU NEED TO KNOW

What Is Quantum Theory?

Quantum theory is the most important, fascinating, challenging, and even mystifying area of science, and it is considerably more than just weird. It is also the most inspiring concept in the world today. The presumption is that we might well be profoundly mistaken in our assumptions as to what truth really is.

Originally, the theory was first christened quantum mechanics, considering it was assumed that there must have been some common laws involved in the activity of atomic particles and quantum energy, similar to the mechanics of the macroscopic subject matter of major planets. The hypothesis attempts to describe the behavior of exceedingly small entities, in general, the magnitude of atoms or smaller, in much the same way that Einstein's theory of relativity describes the laws of more common entities. This is used in other campaigns, including television and PCs, and it also explains nuclear activities in and around the stars.

Quantumists have us living in an infinite number of dimensions furnished in the midst of probability waves and unrecognized virtual particles that flare in and out of existence, but they express verbally that one day we may glide through wormholes within the universe to look around other cosmoses or to fly backward in time. In much simpler terms, quantum theory is the analysis of the leaps from one energy echelon to another, as it refers to the fabric and behavior of the atoms.

In 1905, Albert Einstein proposed that light was a particle and not a wave, questioning a hundred years of research. He conjectured that not just the energy but the radiation itself was quantified in the same way. This is the root of Einstein's well-known statement that "God does not play dice." Einstein certainly could not embrace it as an accomplished science, seeing that quantum mechanics may well, in general, only bestow probabilities on how individual particles react, and it does not work out certain certainties. For this reason, despite his many novel approximations, Einstein could never let go of the purpose of pre-quantum science to be competent to predict the cosmos like clockwork. Quantum science is not, as Einstein thought, an incomplete science, but, in reality, it is a rather pragmatic science, inasmuch as it recognizes that in complicated techniques, science will at most give rise to expectations for the reaction of distinct divisions.

Unquestionably, quantum theory and Albert Einstein's theory of relativity form the basis of modern-day physics, with almost every person conceiving that it is, in fact, the theory of the imperceptible sphere, of tiny particles, and of enormous accelerators. For most people, however, this is a slogan for enigmatic, unfathomable science. This does, however, have a much wider range than just the diminutive sphere and can be adapted to strategies in which several separate parts work with each other while also influencing each other.

Max Planck: Creator of Quantum Theory

The man who created this field of study was the German physicist Max Planck. He published his famous work on black body radiation, which stated that radiant energy could be emitted only in discrete amounts of high energy, called *quanta.*

Quanta is often described as "packets" of light or other types of energy that are released in a steady stream over time, rather than all at once. This idea is one primary basis for quantum theory, but it also has important implications for the way that subatomic particles are modeled within the mathematics of quantum theory.

The origin of quantum theory can be traced back to a paper written by Planck in 1900. In this paper, he described his theory on the nature of light as waves. However, he believed that these waves were not able to be transmitted through a solid object—they were simply a series of infinitesimally small waves that emitted from an object over time without ever reaching their mark at all.

However, shortly before this paper was published, one of Planck's students published a paper suggesting that light could be considered vibrations in some material. Planck was quite troubled by this and set out to correct his student's theory. He began by extending his original model to assume that light waves could be considered as particles as well as waves—and this is where the origin of quantum theory truly began.

For the next several years, Planck worked diligently on his theory and eventually came up with a set of three principles:

The first principle stated that light energy was emitted in small amounts; this would later come to be known as Planck's constant. Planck believed that if you were to look at something emitting light over time, the amount of energy you would see coming from it would be absorbed by increasing increments, but never any larger than these quanta.

Black Body Radiation

The second law stated that the energy released by heat radiation was proportional to the fourth power of absolute temperature. This means that if you were to take any object and increase its temperature, you would be able to see a rise in energy levels. However, this rise would be relatively minor at first and far more significant towards the end.

The third law stated that an object's energy levels could never fall below a certain point, referred to as zero-point energy. This law greatly simplified the calculations needed to predict an object's amount of available energy based on its temperature.

These three principles helped establish quantum theory as a comprehensive and robust model system for analyzing the nature of light, heat, and other forms of radiation through precise mathematical studies.

Photoelectric Effect

This theory also played a factor in developing the photoelectric effect, which explains how electrons are ejected from atoms when energy is applied. In the early 1900s, Planck was able to use his theory, combined with his experimental work on radiation, to explain the photoelectric effect.

Planck found that he could explain all these findings by assuming that light quanta were emitted from a hotter object and then absorbed more quickly as the object cooled down. He had essentially introduced a model for light particle emission and absorption based on Planck's constant.

Compton Effect

This led to the development of another great theory in quantum theory, named after American physicist Earnest Arthur Compton. It describes how radiation interacts with matter, and it explains the results that were observed when scientists studied the H-R diagram. This is commonly referred to as an "energy spectrum," but it's actually a plot of emission versus absorption.

Compton found that he could relate this spectrum to Planck's data on black body radiation, giving him a way to predict the amount of light released by any object based on its temperature. He also concluded that an object was emitting light if it absorbed energy from other objects in its vicinity.

Atomic Model of Bohr-Sommerfeld

This idea would later be expanded upon by Danish physicist Niels Bohr, who introduced a model for the atom that explained the emission and absorption of photons. It stated that electrons could only exist at certain orbits around the nucleus and that you couldn't detect them without firing off a photon. Once the photon was fired off, it would either be reflected or transmitted, and then absorbed or released as another photon by another object. This theory is now known as Bohr's model of the atom.

Bohr's Atomic Model

This model also introduced the idea of quantum jumps and states. A quantum jump was used to describe the jump of an electron from one orbit to another, while a quantum state referred to any distinct position within an atomic orbit.

The Bohr model was never widely accepted, though. For one thing, it only accounted for the lower energy world of an atom. Bohr's model also stated that atoms are made up of subatomic particles with a matrix to hold them together, but scientists could not find this particle.

Hertz Model

To correct these problems, physicists soon began working on a new model by another Dane named Hans Christian Oersted. He believed that electrons could not be bound to specific orbits around the nucleus—they could jump from place to place by vibrating between different orbitals, depending on the amount of energy applied to them. This idea is now known as the Hertz model.

The Sommerfeld Quantization

Oersted also came up with plans for how his theory could be used to predict the amount of energy emitted by an atom based on the temperature of the object. He was able to predict this by using Planck's formula to determine the amount of radiation absorbed or released. However, he didn't take into account Planck's constant.

Niels Bohr took this failure into account and developed his own theory that accounted for Planck's constant. This new model was called *the Sommerfeld quantization*, and it showed that atoms were not made up of subatomic particles; they were instead composed of energy quanta that simultaneously existed in many different states at once.

He also introduced the idea that energy levels could

be divided into minima and maxima, with minima being lower in energy, and maxima being higher. The maxima can be thought of as the absolute maximum states that an energy level can exist in.

Wave-Particle Dualism

This worked well and was able to explain the results of electrons orbiting within atomic orbits. However, it failed to explain the photoelectric effect. This led physicists to work on a new model by Max Born, and it became known as the wave-particle dualism model.

Born realized that he could use the photon as a carrier for quantum energy—just like an electron—and that it would be absorbed or released by objects in its path. However, he still couldn't fully explain this process due to Planck's constant still being unaccounted for.

This led to the creation of an equation that would explain the constant by Max Planck's younger cousin, Louis de Broglie. He introduced a new version of Planck's constant, which is called *the Planck-Broglie wavelength*.

He stated that the Planck-Broglie wavelength could be used to calculate any amount of energy based on its frequency. This allowed for more precise equations predicting the amount of energy released by an atom based on its temperature.

The De Broglie Hypothesis

The De Broglie hypothesis is an equation describing the relationship between the Planck-Broglie wavelength and quantum energy. It states that since the Planck-Broglie wavelength is equal to the product of the frequency of an object's radiation and Planck's constant, then it can be used to predict the amount of energy released by any object.

Any object releasing radiation will eventually have its light absorbed by another object, be it a human eye or a thermometer. When this happens, one of two things will result: the object could absorb the light in full, leaving nothing for anyone else to see, or it could reflect some of its light off onto someone else.

The Two-Slits Experiment

This is where the famous two-slits experiment comes into play. In the experiment, two slits are cut into a large screen, and a source of light is aimed at it from behind. Then, a photographic plate records where any particles of light hit it.

Physicist Hendrik Lorentz took this data and came up with a formula that predicted where the particles of light should hit the plate based on the number of openings in the screen and how far away they were from one another. He found that if he was to repeat his experiment with electrons instead of photons, he would get an entirely different result than what he saw in his experiment with photons.

CHAPTER 3: SCHRODINGER EQUATION

Schrodinger's equation is a wave equation that describes the quantum mechanical state of a physical system. It is commonly used as a model for nuclear physics and quantum mechanics. In place of classical mechanics, it allows for the simultaneous existence of multiple states whose superpositions—or more generally, probabilities—vanish if measured.

Schrodinger's equation is widely used in physics, chemistry, and mathematics, as well as in popular culture to explain physical phenomena such as nuclear fission and radioactive decay, laser cooling, entanglement, and decoherence.

The equation is named after Schrodinger, although the term *wave function* was used earlier in discussions of wave mechanics by Max Born. In 1935, Born and Werner Heisenberg showed that quantum mechanics could be formulated using matrices and vectors. They also developed the mathematical formalism of matrix mechanics, which predicted that action at a distance is possible and described bonds and forces in molecules and atomic nuclei.

When Schrodinger discovered the equation in late 1925, he wrote to Wolfgang Pauli: "I have written a paper on a problem in quantum theory, and the paper will probably appear in Naturwissenschaften. I myself regard it as my most important work ever" (Schrödinger 1925). The theory and application of 10 years of his life was his "most important work ever."

Schrodinger's equation captures well the counterintuitive nature of quantum mechanics. Although not itself one of the tenets of quantum mechanics, it is often thought to be part of the Copenhagen interpretation (although not universally accepted).

To solve the wave function, we need to know what that function is. The problem is that we do not know, and the only thing we can do is guess. We use tools such as mathematics and probability theory to base our guesses on reasoning and experience of complex systems.

The Schrodinger equation describes how a physical system behaves in quantum physics. It says that, in order to find out its exact state, we must measure all the relevant properties of the system at the same time:

It turns out that each property has a characteristic time "t" at which it can be measured. If the state of the system changes between measurements, then we cannot know all its properties simultaneously. Therefore, quantum physics predicts that a particle does not have a well-defined position and momentum simultaneously. The best you can hope for is an uncertainty relation that limits how accurately you can know both of them simultaneously.

According to the Copenhagen interpretation, the wave function is not just a tool for predicting probabilities, but rather it is an actual physical entity. Physical systems do not have objectively predetermined values of physical properties, but rather they are defined by and evolve dynamically through measurement and observation (which sometimes collapses the wave function). At the same time, every observation causes a quantum level change in the state of the system observed, which then evolves according to Schrodinger's equation.

The physical interpretation of the wave function is that it is a probability distribution for all aspects of the system, corresponding to an approximate description of the state of the system. This interpretation implies that there are no real substantial entities in the world, only probability distributions.

For example, so-called virtual particles can be added to a theory to help specify other properties, for example, force carriers that carry forces between other particles. They are not real particles but rather just probability distributions for various properties. The fact that they can be added to a theory without changing its predictions is independent of quantum mechanics and has been known since Newton's time.

CHAPTER 4: THE CAT AND THE SUPERPOSITION

The Superposition Principle

The superposition principle is one of the most essential concepts in quantum physics—one that needs to be properly understood because it lies at the foundation of many quantum applications.

That sounds a bit complicated, but what the superposition principle implies, in fact, is that, in quantum physics, a particle can exist in all states at once, so they can move at different speeds and have different energies all at the same time.

This happens because, as has been mentioned before, particles behave both like waves and particles at the same time. If you think of two ocean waves coming together, and you consider them as a collection of particles, you can either see them clashing and annihilating each other or coming together in a new state (i.e., a bigger wave), which is how traditional physics saw the interaction between two waves (and which is also the theory upon which numerous applications were built, including noise-canceling headphones, for example).

In quantum physics, the superposition principle feels rather counterintuitive for anyone coming from traditional physics, precisely because it assumes that a dynamic system can exist in all states, but that the "general state" is given by the overlapping of two or more states (where the general state is defined as what you actually see, or the state that is measured).

Basically, the superposition principle shows that everything is possible at the same time and that the act of measurement (as it is preponderantly understood in the Copenhagen interpretation) is precisely what makes a particular something happen. Needless to say, this comes with a lot of real-life implications because it removes linearity from an equation.

One of the best real-life implications that come with this is quantum computing, which relies a lot on the superposition principle. In traditional computing, humans and machines communicate with each other through a series of codes made up of zeros and ones. In this context, you can only work with zeros and ones alternatively. In quantum computing, however, due to the principle of superposition, you can work with zeros and ones simultaneously.

The consequences of this are tremendous, and they are to be applied in a series of real-life technological improvements. For example, it is believed that quantum computing is one of the most important elements in developing advanced artificial intelligence (yes, like the one you see in the movies).

Schrödinger's Cat

Let's face it: the internet is enamored with cats and everything they do. Every cat is famous these days, but in the world of science, there is no cat more famous than... Schrödinger's cat.

If you have heard of the term, it means you had at least a bit of tangential interaction with quantum physics. We hate to disappoint, though, and say that this concept has nothing to do with an actual cat (unlike in the famous example with Pavlov's dog, for example).

What Schrödinger's cat refers to, in fact, is a thought experiment (or a thinking exercise, if you want to call it this way) proposed by Schrödinger (and preceded by Albert Einstein).

In this paradoxical thought experiment, Schrödinger describes a cat that is locked in a steel chamber with a radioactive atom and a flask of poison that the radioactive atom might spill. The cat may or may not die, depending on whether the radioactive atom is decayed or still emitting radiation. However, the state of the cat is not known until it is observed, so until someone opens the steel chamber to see if the cat is dead or alive, the cat exists in both states, both dead and alive.

Oddly enough, Schrödinger's cat example was meant to contradict the Copenhagen interpretation of the "act of measurement" and point out how ridiculous it seems to think that a photon or a particle can exist in all possible states until it is measured and collapses into a state.

Instead of surviving as a counterexample (and, by all initial intents and purposes, a mock) of the superposition principle proposed by quantum physics, Schrödinger's cat slowly started to be associated with it. Today, the cat example is given every time quantum physicists explain the superposition principle, and experiments show that the superposition principle might just be true.

Furthermore, the famous cat (thought) experiment gave birth to new interpretations and explanations as well.

● In the Copenhagen interpretation, the cat becomes dead or alive when the box is opened.

● In the Many Worlds interpretation, the cat is both dead and alive once the box is open because the observer becomes entangled with the cat and splits into two states (an observer looking at a dead cat and one looking at a cat that is alive). However, because the two observers are decoherent, they do not interact with each other.

● In the relational interpretation, every participant is an observer. For instance, the cat becomes an observer of the apparatus (the box and the atom with the flask of poison) and the human becomes an observer of the system (the cat and the apparatus).

Until the box is opened, the two have different information about the reality, but when the box is opened, the two observers' realities "collapse" and become one.

● In the transactional interpretation, the apparatus (the box and the atom) sends an advanced wave back in time. At the same time, the source sends a wave forward in time. The two waves are combined, and the apparatus becomes an observer. The collapse of the wave function is atemporal, and it happens across the entire transaction between the source and the apparatus. As such, the cat is never in superposition; it is only in one state at a particular time, regardless of what the human does. In conclusion, the transactional interpretation resolves the quantum paradox.

● In the Zeno effect interpretation, the environment becomes the so-called "observer." The human may peek into the box sooner or later, but the state of the cat is either delayed or accelerated due to its environment (i.e., the atom and the flask of poison).

● In the objective collapse interpretation, superpositions are destroyed instantaneously when a specific objective physical threshold (time, mass, etc.) is reached. As such, the cat dies or continues to live long before the box is opened and its state is observed.

Who would have known that a cat could generate so much debate in the scientific community? And yet, here we are. The famous Schrödinger's cat example is still being discussed to date, and there is no unanimous response to the problem. However, what remains a fact is that quantum physicists all agree that the cat is (at least in a sense) both alive and dead until the state is observed. In other words, you, as an observer, will not know if the cat is alive or dead until you open the box to see it with your own eyes.

Understanding how to maneuver this situation is bound to attract a whole new series of practical applications in quantum physics—some of which are, as you will see, quite the science fiction scenarios.

CHAPTER 5: HEISENBERG UNCERTAINTY PRINCIPLE, ARE YOU READY TO FLY?

66 Anyone who is not surprised by quantum theory has not understood it," said Niels Bohr, a pivotal contributor to quantum mechanics theory.

Such is the beauty of entanglement theory; as more and more years go by, and as more and more scientists get their hands on it, they have to find new ways of explaining their shortcomings—the uncertainty principle is the most prominent.

Also called the Heisenberg uncertainty principle and the indeterminacy principle, the uncertainty principle states that there is no exact measurement of the position or velocity of an object in the quantum world. The concept of exactness has no place in this realm, not even in theory.

The uncertainty principle regards only tiny objects as immeasurable because it applies to the quantum world. For this reason, ordinary objects do not apply to the uncertainty principle. There is proof of this: any person can find an exact measurement of a car because they can weigh it. It is ordinary and, therefore, large enough to be accurately pinpointed.

Even a category of tiny objects qualifies for more accurate measurement than the uncertainty principle makes a room. These objects are ones whose velocity and position are equal to or greater than Planck's constant, 6.6 x 10^-34 joule-second. Small items below Planck's constant apply to the uncertainty principle.

The uncertainty principle arose from classic wave-particle duality. Every particle has an accompanying wave. The more undulating that lock is, the more uncertain its measurement is. The more specific its accompanying particle's position, the more indefinite its momentum.

Heisenberg also made another significant contribution to quantum mechanics in 1927. He argued that because matter behaves like waves, some properties, such as the position and speed of the electron, are complementary, implying that there is a limit (related to the Planck constant) to how well the accuracy and property can be understood. Under what would come to be called the *Heisenberg theory of uncertainty*, it was argued that the more precisely the electron's position is determined, the less precisely its speed can be known, and vice versa. This uncertainty theory often applies to everyday objects but is not apparent since the lack of precision is too high.

Werner Heisenberg (1901–1976) was the theorists' prince. He was so disinterested in laboratory practice that he risked flunking his thesis at the University of Munich because he did not know how batteries worked. Fortunately for him, and for physics as a whole, he was also promoted. There were other difficult moments in his life. During the First World War, while his father was at the front as a soldier, the scarcity of food and fuel in the city was such that schools and universities were often forced to suspend classes. And in the summer of 1918, young Werner, weakened and malnourished, was forced together with other students to help the farmers on a Bavarian farm harvest.

With the end of the war, in the first years of the twenties, we find him in the shoes of the young prodigy: pianist of high level poured in the classical languages, skillful skier and alpinist, as well as mathematician of rank lent to the physics. During lessons with his old teacher Arnold Sommerfeld, he met another promising young man, Wolfgang Pauli, who would later become his closest collaborator and his fiercest critic. In 1922, Sommerfeld took the

21-year-old Heisenberg to Göttingen. The beacon of European science attended a series of lectures dedicated to the nascent quantum atomic physics, given by Niels Bohr himself. On that occasion, the young researcher, not intimidated, dared to counter some guru statements and challenges at the root of his theoretical model. However, after this first confrontation, a long and fruitful collaboration was born, marked by mutual admiration.

From that moment, Heisenberg devoted himself body and soul to the enigmas of quantum mechanics. In 1924, he spent some time in Copenhagen working directly with Bohr on radiation emission and absorption problems. There he learned to appreciate the "philosophical attitude" (in Pauli's words) of the great Danish physicist. Frustrated by the difficulties to make concrete the atomic model of Bohr, with its orbits put in that way, who knows how the young man was convinced that there must be something wrong at the root. The more he thought about it, the more it seemed to him that those simple, almost circular orbits were a surplus, a purely intellectual construct. To get rid of them, he began to think that the very idea of rotation was a Newtonian residue that had to be done.

The young Werner imposed on himself a fierce

doctrine: no model could be based on classical physics (so no miniature solar systems, even if they were so cute to draw). The way to salvation was not intuition or aesthetics but mathematical rigor. Another of his conceptual digits was the renunciation of all entities (such as orbits, in fact) that could not be measured directly.

Measurable in the atoms were the spectral lines, the witness of photons' emission or absorption by the particles resulting from jumping between the electron levels. So it was to those net, visible, and verifiable lines corresponding to the inaccessible subatomic world that Heisenberg turned his attention. To solve this diabolically complicated problem and to find relief from hay fever, in 1925, he retired to Helgoland, a remote island in the North Sea.

His starting point was the so-called "correspondence principle," enunciated by Bohr, according to which quantum laws had to be transformed without problems into the corresponding classical rules when applied to sufficiently large systems. But how big? Enough to allow for the neglect of the Planck constant h in the relative equations. A typical object of the atomic world has a mass equal to 10–27 kg; let's consider that a grain of dust barely visible to the naked eye can weigh 10–7 kg: very little, but it is still more significant by a factor of 100000000000000, that is 1020, one followed by twenty zeros. So, the atmospheric dust is clearly in the domain of classical physics—it is a macroscopic object. Its motion is not affected by the presence of factors dependent on Planck's constant. The fundamental quantum laws apply naturally to the phenomena of the atomic and subatomic world. Simultaneously, it loses sense to use them to describe phenomena related to aggregates larger than atoms as the dimensions grow, and quantum physics gives way to the classical laws of Newton and Maxwell. The foundation of this principle (as we will repeat several times) is that the strange and unpublished quantum effects "correspond" directly to the classical concepts of physics as you leave the atomic field to enter the macroscopic one.

Driven by Bohr's ideas, Heisenberg redefined the banalest notions of classical physics in a quantum field as the position and velocity of an electron. They were in correspondence with the Newtonian equivalents. But he soon realized that his reconciliation efforts between two worlds led to the birth of a new and bizarre "algebra of physics."

In school, we all learned the so-called commutative property of multiplication. Given any two numbers a and b, their product does not change if we exchange them between them; in symbols: a×b=b×a. It is evident, for example, that 3×4 =4×3=12. However, in Heisenberg's time, abstract numerical systems in commutative property did not always apply. It is not said that a × b is equal to b × a. Examples of non-commutative operations are also found in nature. A classic case is rotations and tilts (try to perform two different wheels on an object like a book, and you will find examples where the order they happen is essential).

CHAPTER 6:
ENTANGLEMENT AND EPR PARADOX

What is Entanglement?

The phrase "entanglement" refers to the phenomenon of a physical system's behavior in response to nearby interactions, such as two electrons being affected by all the other particles in their vicinity. This is because all these particles are yet another level of "small-world connectivity".

The important lesson here is that whenever a system interacts with its surrounding world, it will always be entangled with those objects. Our world has plenty of entanglements that we can theorize exist between our minds and our bodies, or even inside each cell in our body.

In mathematics, the term "entanglement" is defined more precisely as follows:

"A system of two or more particles, which can be in a state of quantum superposition (that is, an infinite number of possible states), and which are entangled. Two or more such systems constitute a quantum state".

It seems to me that this definition demonstrates that our bodies, brains and consciousness are all quantum systems.

Why do we care about this particular kind of entanglement?

Our bodies, brains and consciousness are all entangled with our immediate environment – the world around us. We cannot exist without them at some level.

All of our knowledge is dependent upon this entanglement.

In the equation that defines QM, the knowledge of measurement results is a "hidden variable" that exists in all entangled states. But what is the source of this entanglement?

Entanglement and locality are incompatible. The two are different sides of quantum physics' coin. Even though both exist simultaneously, they are incompatible with each other. If we confirm one side (i.e., entanglement), we must sacrifice the other (i.e., locality).

In quantum entanglement experiments, we can see from the results that "pure" quantum states are not independent of their environment. The questions that remain for researchers are:

1) Why does this entanglement occur?

2) How does it arise?

3) Can we describe all hidden variables and the nature of reality in QM through mathematics?

These questions have been researched and debated by generations, spanning over a century. Some have suggested that all particles collapse into a single wave function when they interact, and that our minds are both in the present and their pasts (i.e., "retrocausality").

Others have suggested that entanglement doesn't exist and that there is no such thing as a "quantum mind".

The question of how entanglement can arise in the first place has been researched using the Schrodinger equation. The researchers propose that, after the interaction of one particle with the environment, the other particle will inherit this new state. Thus, this process is continuous and does not require a sudden collapse into any particular state.

Whether quantum states are real can be answered using Bell's theorem. This helps scientists to confirm whether there is a hidden variable, or a new state that we, contained in the system cannot observe. If so, then this means that the particle experiments demonstrate the existence of another new state.

We have to acknowledge a new state – the entanglement – along with the measurable results. This means that:

1) The two-particle entangled state exists before and after the measurement and we cannot peer into it during measurement (this is called "locality").

2) The universe exists before and after our measurements (this is called "realism").

Those who obey the laws of locality and realism are labeled "local realism", while those who violate locality are labeled "superrealism".

The Copenhagen interpretation of QM has already represented a clear violation of locality and realism, but it becomes impossible to agree with local realism if we include the entanglement.

Researchers have provided an alternative theory to avoid this problem: the theory of "many worlds".

This new approach essentially rewrites history to explain how "entangled states can exist in different worlds simultaneously". In other words, we must make our measurements in different worlds simultaneously.

The theory implies a connection between these

different worlds, and that our reality is an illusion. It can also answer the question: What is the actual nature of these "other worlds", and why do we not observe them?

This topic has already received extensive attention in popular science (e.g., philosophy of science, physics fiction), literature, art and music.

Theorists have proposed that, along with the "many worlds", there is a virtual reality (VR) universe behind our own. The VR universe is only a simulation that humans can never observe in real life.

Many science fiction writers have introduced this idea (e.g., Philip K Dick, Robert J Sawyer) and philosophers (e.g., Nick Bostrom). It has also been explored in "The Matrix" series.

Many scientists have also suggested that this may explain why VR is possible for us, such as David Chalmers and John Searle. They are experts in philosophy of mind and consciousness respectively.

The core of this theory is a layer that lies between the "real" world and the human brain, which acts as an interface. This layer contains all the programs in our brain and records every moment we experience in VR.

Since we never observe any of these other worlds,

this information about them is assumed to be lost –
just like how we can only perceive our world.

Our perception of reality might just be a simulation
created by this VR program, or a "false reality". We
live inside a simulation instead of the real universe,
and don't know it because we can only perceive this
virtual world. The world that we are imagining and
experiencing is within our brain.

CHAPTER 7:
WHAT EXACTLY
IS QUANTUM
TUNNELING?

Q uantum tunneling is a process where an object that does not have enough energy to pass through an area (i.e., a barrier), "borrows" energy from somewhere else and uses it to pass through the barrier anyway even though it wouldn't have from its stores of energy alone. This is one way that atoms can be in two places at once.

But, how does this happen and why does it happen?

It all starts with the wave function, a mathematical representation of an object's location (or momentum) at any instant of time. Atoms are made up of a sea of particles called quarks, bound together into composite particles called protons and neutrons. The way that atoms get their energy to carry out their chemical reactions is by having some sort of "arrow" that points towards where they want to go. These arrows or quanta come in two flavors: positive (up) and negative (down). For example, the neutron has a positive arrow towards its proton, so it combines with that proton. Likewise, a proton has a negative arrow away from that neutron, so it wants to combine

59

with the neutron.

This combination is called fusing and when it happens, energy is usually released in the process. This is the energy source for all chemical reactions happening on Earth (and pretty much anywhere else). The real question is how those arrows get to point towards where they point. And this is where quantum tunneling comes into play.

So, if you take two protons with positive and negative arrows towards their partner neutrons and put them close enough together, the arrows will begin to overlap at their tips. So, in this case, the protons have one arrow "inside" and the other "outside" of them. This means that there is not enough energy for these protons to separate into their original state. So, instead, they will only be able to pass through each other's presence (in some cases only a small amount of energy will manage this). This is called "quantum tunneling".

Two protons with positive and negative arrows are shown above merging. If they overlap too much, they will become unstable and collapse into a neutron-proton combination and release an enormous amount of energy in the process.

On the other hand, if you took two protons with arrows away from each other and put them close enough together, the arrows would pass through each other without touching. This is exactly how an alpha particle (which is 2 protons clumped together with 2 neutrons) got its energy to overcome gravity and escape from the nucleus of an atom in the first place. So, it is as if there was no arrow at all in this case, and this gives energy to things that wouldn't have it otherwise.

This type of tunneling doesn't happen with neutrons because they have no charge against which they could tunnel. They are also very heavy and there is no energy that they can get from somewhere else to overcome their mass. However, if you take an electron, which has a positive charge on its "inside" end and a negative charge on its "outside" end, it can tunnel through anything no matter how small the barrier is. This means that there will be energy that isn't available to electrons at the barrier to get through with their borrowed energy.

This is why atoms have all kinds of different shapes and sizes. If they were all the same size, all of their borrowed energy would have the same amount of push behind it so none of them would be able to tunnel through each other.

The human body also has to deal with tunneling when it comes to food and oxygen intake. Our cells take in the energy of food by sucking it in through the cell membrane (a very thin layer that acts as a barrier, stopping the water in our cells from flowing out) and letting it pack into the cell. Once it has packed, the cell wants to expel it all back into our blood system. But this isn't easy because there is a barrier in our blood system that acts as a barrier (one of the various things I call "blood work"). The cell doesn't need the energy itself; it just needs enough energy to function. So, the cell will take in that energy using tunneling and store it for later use.

This happens between every step of a chemical reaction we take as well. Even if the chemical reaction isn't a chemical reaction at all, it still takes energy to pull an electron over a barrier. For example, think of the food that you swallow and how it is digested in the stomach. That food has gained the electrons we ate and pumped them into our cells. But there are barriers to this process (referred to as "gates" in digestion research) that prevent those electrons from being able to tunnel back out of our cells. So, instead, they are only able to tunnel back through these gates when we take in energy from something else (typically eating more food). So, the food you've eaten will take the electrons from your cells, store them up and use them later to transform into nutrients you need to grow.

CHAPTER 8: STRING THEORY

T here's a good chance that, as a reader of this book, you've heard of the term *string theory*, but you have no idea what it means. As it turns out, this is the case for many people, and not by their own fault, either—string theory is just really, really confusing.

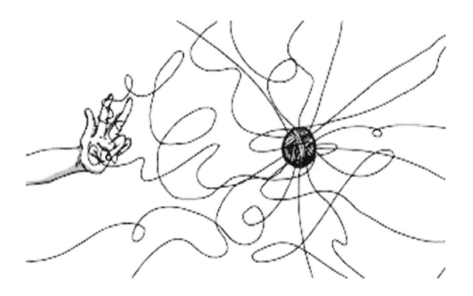

String theory is so named because it was created to describe the nature of quantum objects as something like a vibrating string, and those objects were measured based on those vibrations. Without getting too deeply into it—string theory involves a lot of work with subatomic particles, which are the smaller particles that make up atoms (like quarks, for example)—string theory was essentially formulated to help explain strange interactions that sometimes happen between some of the known subatomic particles. These particles sometimes act like they are bound together by strings. Thus, string theory was formed.

Now, one of the most exciting parts of this early string theory was that these weird, string-based interactions worked out some really mysterious math. For one, the vibrations in the strings predicted the existence of a certain particle: the graviton. It's the only quantum theory that has been able to successfully do this so far. Theoretically, a graviton is a particle that causes gravity, and one of string theory's most significant advantages here is that its graviton is actually shaped like a donut. That may sound strange, but that shape prevents many of the mathematical anomalies that arise when trying to envision gravity as a particle. However, with today's science, we still can't prove that the graviton exists—gravity still presents many mysteries.

String theory was able to successfully describe gravity as its own quantum particle this way. However, string theory has many limitations that keep it from being an attractive (or logical) solution to the mysteries of the quantum universe. For one, the final proposal of string theory requires ten dimensions to function correctly, but we've so far only observed four dimensions in our existence. To remedy that, physicists and scientists alike have tried to make string theory work in its prerequisite ten dimensions, and then remove the extra dimensions that don't apply to our universe. However, none have yet been successful. In addition, there are several other versions of string theory—there isn't just one! Bosonic string theory is one example, and it requires twenty-six dimensions.

In 1995, a man named Ed Witten managed to combine many of the varied string theories into one, which he dubbed M-theory. However, M-theory required eleven dimensions, so while it managed to unify many of the past string theories into one neat package, it still didn't seem anywhere near good science. (It's also very complicated and unnecessary for us to analyze here.)

This doesn't mean that string theory isn't useful. There's also a concept out there called the *theory of everything*, and, as the name implies, this is an all-encompassing theory to explain how quantum physics and quantum particles work. Although it's one of the premier goals of today's physicists and scientists, we haven't formulated a working theory of everything yet. However, string theory makes a compelling case for becoming, or at least supplementing, a potential theory of everything.

For one, string theory makes a very neat argument for explaining the nature of particles. Envision a guitar string in slow motion: the string moves in a wave shape, just like light or sound. The tension (how taut the string is pulled) of the string also controls what note any string on a guitar plays. If you pluck the string, it will vibrate. This is the prevailing theory behind the strings: each string has a different frequency (like the note of a guitar string) that it vibrates at, and each string also has a different length, which changes the number of notes the string could possibly play. Think about how, when playing the guitar, moving your fingers down the neck will shorten and play higher notes while moving your hand up the neck will lengthen the string and play lower notes. Interestingly enough, the intervals between these possible "notes" are also defined by a familiar variable: Planck's constant.

Unfortunately, as convenient as this might seem, there's one question that scientists seem to be unwilling (or unable) to answer about string theory. What are the strings made of? Answers that have been tried are "pure mass" (whatever that means), irregularities in the fabric of reality, and the "energy" of "existence." The best answer, however, is "the answer is irrelevant because they're there."

One of the biggest downfalls of string theory is that, because it's so complicated and exists in so many additional dimensions (that we can't even find), we can't test it. However, we also can't rule it out as entirely wrong, either. This creates a bit of a catch twenty-two: should scientists and physicists keep pouring manhours and research into a theory that we technically can't even test, or should we just give up on it and risk sidelining a potential theory of the universe? There's no good answer to this question, but it's one of the pitfalls that plagues string theory and those interested in it.

Despite its shortcomings, many scientists still believe that string theory is the way things are—or, at least, it's a step to figuring things out. However, until we find six or seven more dimensions, we'll have to wait on that.

CHAPTER 9: QUANTUM COMPUTING

Is Information Physical?

Computers are devices that process information. Computer scientist and physicist Rolf Landauer argued that knowledge is a part of the physical world. He elaborated on this theory: Data is not a disembodied abstract entity; it is always linked to physical representation. It is shown by engraving on a stone tablet, a turn (magnetic), a charge (electrical), a hole in a punched card, a mark on paper, or some other equivalents. It links the handling of information with all the possibilities and limitations of our actual physical world, its physics laws, and its storage of parts. If "information is physical," as Landauer has said, then it would seem necessary to treat it mechanically. The physical means by which information is stored and interpreted by computers should be considered using quantum theory. It helps to understand computation before addressing quantum computers.

What Is a Computer?

A computer is a technology that receives and stores information input, processes the information according to a programmable sequence of steps, and produces the resulting output of information. The term *computer* was used for the first time in the 1600s to refer to people who perform calculations or computations; now it refers to computers that compute. Computing machines can be divided roughly into 4 types, detailed below.

Computing devices for classical computational physics: These machines use moving parts, including levers and gears, to perform computing. Usually, they are not programmable but always perform the same operation, such as adding numbers. An example is the 1905 Burroughs adding machine.

Electromechanical classical mechanics fully programmable computing devices: These machines operate using electronically controlled moving parts. They process information stored as digital bits represented by the locations of a large number of electromechanical switches.

The first such machine was built in 1941 by Konrad Zuse in wartime Germany. In theory, their programmability allows them to solve any problem found and overcome by using algebra. These were the first "universal" computers in this context.

All-electronic, hybrid quantum-classical-physics computers: These fully programmable, universal computing machines have no moving mechanical parts and work using electronic circuits. The first to be constructed was the ENIAC, engineered by John Mauchly and J. Presper Eckert, University of Pennsylvania, 1946. The physical principles that describe electrons' motion in these circuits are rooted in quantum physics. But, given that there are no superposition states or entangled states involving electrons in different circuit components (capacitors, transistors, etc.), classical physics adequately describes how electrons represent information. Therefore, we call these machines—practically any computer in operation today—*classic computers*.

Quantum computers: If ever built successfully, these devices would operate according to quantum physics principles. Knowledge will be expressed by the quantum states of individual electrons or other elementary quantum artifacts, and there will be entangled states involving electrons in various circuit components. These computers are expected to solve those kinds of problems much faster than any modern classical computer can.

How Do Computers Work?

Computers store and manipulate information using a binary alphabet language consisting of only 2 symbols: 0 and 1. Every 1 or 0 characters is referred to as a bit, short for a binary digit because it can take one of two possible values. A page of text is represented as a long string of numbers in a computer file. A binary code represents every letter. For example, "A" becomes 01000001, "B" becomes 01000010, and so on.

Each bit is represented by the number of electrons stored in a small device called a *typical computer's capacitor*. We can imagine a capacitor as a box that holds a certain number of electrons, sort of like a bulk grain bin in a food store that carries a certain amount of rice. Each capacitor is called a *memory cell*. For example, such a capacitor could have a maximum capacity of 1,000 electrons. If the capacitor is full or almost full of electrons, we say it represents a bit value of 1. If the capacitor is empty or nearly empty, we say it represents a bit value of 0. The capacitor is not allowed to be half-filled, and the circuitry is designed to ensure that this does not happen. Through grouping together 8 capacitors, each of which is either full or empty, any 8-bit number— e.g., 01110011—can be interpreted.

According to a set of principles called a program,

the machine circuitry's role is to empty or fill various capacitors. Eventually, the action of filling and emptying the capacitors manages to perform the desired calculation—say, to add 2 8-bit numbers. In a computer, the steps are performed by tiny components of computer circuitry called *logic gates*. A logic gate is made of silicon and other elements arranged to either block or pass electrical charge, depending on its electrical environment. Logic gate inputs are bit values, represented by a full capacitor (a 1) or an empty capacitor (a 0). (The word "gate" is associated with the fact that something goes into it and something comes out of it.)

How Small Can a Single Logic Gate Be?

In the beginning, in all electronic computers, such as the ENIAC, built in the 1940s, a single logic gate was a vacuum tube similar to the amplifier tubes still used today in vintage-style electric guitar amplifiers. Each box was at least the size of your thumb. By 1970, the microcircuit revolution reduced the size of each gate to about one-hundredth of a millimeter. When things get much smaller than this, it is best to measure the length of a unit in nanometers; one nanometer is equal to one-millionth of a millimeter. The size of the gate in 1970 was 10,000 nanometers.

A single silicon atom, which is the main atomic element in computer circuitry, is around 0.2 nanometer in thickness. By 2012, available gates in typical computers had been reduced enough to be spaced apart by as little as 22 nanometers—that is, only about a hundred atoms apart. The gate's actual working area was less than 2.2 nanometers of 10 atoms in thickness. This small size allows you to place a few billion memory locations and entrances in an area the size of your thumbnail.

Having gate sizes much smaller than those dimensions leads to both a curse and a blessing. We leave the domain of many-atomic physics and enter the realm of single-atomic physics. There are now variations between the classical physics principles that sufficiently explain the average behavior of many atoms and the quantum physics principles required when dealing with single atoms. We reach a random action domain that does not sound good if we are trying to get a well-regulated system to do our numerical bidding. In reality, a group of scientists led by Michelle Simmons, director of the Center for Quantum Computation and Communication at the University of New South Wales, Australia, constructed a gate comprising a single phosphorus atom placed in a silicon crystal tube. It is the only minor gate ever to be designed. This gate only functions if cooled to shallow temperature: -459°F

(-273°C). Suppose the material is not as cold. In that case, the random (thermal) motion of the silicon atoms in the crystal decreases the confinement of the electron psi wave, which may leak out the channel into which it is confined. For day-to-day desktop computers, which have to operate at room temperature, this leakage prevents such single-atom gates from being the basis of the technology that everyone can use. These experiments show how computers can, at least in theory, be built on the atomic scale, where quantum physics rules.

Can We Create Computers That Use Quantum Behavior?

Given that physics defines the ultimate behavior and efficiency of information transfer, storage, and processing, it is reasonable to ask how quantum physics plays a role in information technology. Because electronic computers are based on the behavior of electrons, and communication systems are based on the behavior of photons, both elementary particles, it is not surprising that quantum physics ultimately determines the performance of information technology. But here is subtlety. Computer technologies currently in use do not involve quantum superposition states to represent information. They use conditions that can be classical forms of material things—namely, groups of electrons.

The big question is: Can we create computers that use quantum-mechanical states to enhance our ability to solve real-world problems? If we ever built such computers, they would bypass specific data encryption methods much faster than any laptop operating today. It would revolutionize privacy and confidentiality for computers and for the internet. The encryption key that might take thousands of years to crack using a conventional computer would only take minutes on a quantum computer.

What Is a Qubit?

The word *bit* refers to both the abstract, disembodied mathematical concept of information and the physical entity that embodies the info. In classical physics, it is clear that a physical bit carries one "abstract bit" of knowledge. There is a straightforward one-to-one relationship between the physical bit's state and the abstract bit's value, 0 or 1. We may also use individual quantum artifacts, such as an electron or a photon, to incarnate a portion. Here, the elementary physical entity is called a *qubit*, short for "quantum bit." A qubit has two different quantum states: the photon's H and V polarization, the upper path, and the electron's lower path. When measured, the results represent a bit value of 0 or 1. But remember that we can select different polarization measurement schemes—say, H/V or D/A. The results may then be random, with the probability of observing likely outcomes depending on which measurement scheme we selected. Here, there was no one-to-one relationship between the state of the physical qubit and the value of some abstract conceptual bit. The concepts of quantum physics suggest significant variations between classical bits and qubits' behavior. Classical bits can be copied as many times as we want, with no degradation of the information; qubits cannot be copied or cloned even once, although they can be teleported. The state of the classical bit, 0 or 1, can be determined by a single measurement; any sequence of measures cannot select the quantum state of the single qubit.

What Physical Principles Differentiate Classically and Quantum Computers Apart?

There are considerable differences between the gates used in classical computers and the gates that need to be used in quantum computers. Classical gates perform operations that are not reversible; understanding the output does not tell you what the inputs are. If a quantum gate is to operate correctly with qubits, it must be reversible. It would help determine the input states by understanding the output states. This requirement arises because any quantum gate operation must be a unit process.

CHAPTER 10: THE FIFTH FORCE OF NATURE

It has opened and continues to widen a glimmer on the dark side of physics, the one that, according to the hopes of the same scientists, could eventually explain all the matter that is still missing in the universe—the dark matter—and the infinitely small subatomic particles to provide the key to explaining the motion of galaxies. The conditional is still a must, but behind an acronym, X17 could hide a new particle, a boson, which could represent a turning point in quantum physics experiments.

A Fifth Physical Force

The known forces that move particles and masses are gravity, electromagnetic, weak interaction, and strong interaction. All four are driven by a vector boson, although the graviton, responsible for the gravitational interaction, has not yet been observed. This quartet explains many observable phenomena in the universe, from the infinitely small to the motion of planets. But, for example, not one of the majority of galaxies that behave as if there was much more mass than we can actually observe: and for this reason, they have called it *dark matter*. A new boson, therefore, could be the one thing driving a force not yet known, and that could explain these anomalies: "If it was a vector boson, like the photon that has spin 1 (responsible for electromagnetism), it could be what is called the dark photon is associated with dark matter in certain theoretical models. And it could add a new force to the standard model. Otherwise, if it had spin 0 (like the Higgs boson, to be clear, which gives mass to particles), it could be a kind of scalar extension of the standard model.

A glimmer on the dark sector.

It could therefore open the door to a new area of fundamental physics: "It is a mechanism of portals, in which the new force would be responsible for the interaction of dark matter with the particles that we already observe—adds the physicist of Infn—the dark sector that 'talks' with the 'normal' sector." But it would not be dark matter itself. The hypothetical boson X17, in fact, decays in a time that is written as a second to minus 14, much, much less than a blink of an eye. A possible particle that gives body to the dark matter should instead be stable.

We have to wait to reach the conclusions. We need new measures, and we need to repeat the experiment to verify what happens at the nuclear level because it could be anomalies related to the nucleus of the atoms of beryllium and helium 4. We are not on scales of energy so high (as that of the Higgs boson to understand ed), but it would be the clue to something new, an extension of the standard model, which has some cracks, but on the whole, it works well.

CHAPTER 11:
QUANTUM PHYSICS IN OUR LIFE

Quantum technologies have increased, and today we cannot drive to grandma's house or buy food without taking advantage of quantum physics. Nevertheless, today's quantum technologies pale in comparison to potential new avenues in the future. The applications of quantum physics to improve health, to create faster computers, and to provide safer communications are on the horizon.

The Neon Light

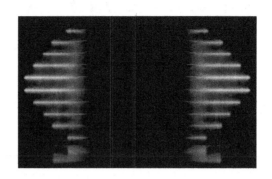

Neon light was first demonstrated in 1855 by the German physicist Heinrich Geissler. He noted that a slight glow was emitted when an electric field was applied through a gas tube containing low-pressure gas.

Nowadays, we know that the applied electric field was stripping the electrons from the atoms in the gas and creating a flow of negative electrons in one direction and positively charged ionized (ions) atoms in the other.

Collisions between fast-flowing ions or electrons with atoms lead to other ionizations, thus continuing the process. This set of electrons and ions is called *plasma*. When we think of solids, liquids, and gases as the only three states of matter, physicists consider plasma as a fourth state.

Collisions between ions or electrons and atoms do not always have enough energy to release atomic electrons. When they do not, colliding atoms are only empowered from their ground state to an excited state. Shortly after that, the atom will transition down to a lowerlying state, thus emitting a photon at a frequency set by the spacing between the energy levels.

These photons are responsible for the glow, and the characteristic frequency defines its color. Red light is emitted when a light discharge uses neon, while helium emits a purple color, carbon dioxide emits a white color, and mercury emits a blue color.

This physical process inspired French engineer Georges Claude to formulate a patent for the technology in France in 1910, which led to the use of neon lights for advertising and art. The light discharge is also the basis of the sodium vapor lamp, whose light yellow-orange glow is used to illuminate many streets around the world.

A miniaturized device that operates on the same principles, the neon incandescent lamp, was introduced in 1917. These were used in the 1970s for electronic displays and today serve as the necessary technology for televisions and plasma displays.

Even ordinary everyday fluorescent bulbs are based on light discharge. Here, the exhaust emissions come from mercury vapor, and these are in the (invisible) range of ultraviolet.

The Laser

The laser is one of the best examples of quantum application because it is widely used.

We have already seen that excited atoms emit photons by making a quantum leap to a lower energy state. In most cases, this occurs without any external influence, and the emissions of this variety are called spontaneous.

This is only half the story since atoms can also be driven to emit photons with a process known as stimulated emission.

Stimulated emission is an essential physical process first envisaged by Einstein in 1917.

Before it became so used, "laser" was an acronym for "light amplification through stimulated emission of radiation."

The first successful laser was developed by the American physicist Theodore Maiman in 1958. He found a similar effect, "microwave amplification by stimulated radiation emission." The short name given to this was the maser, and its realization was awarded the Nobel Prize in 1964.

The stimulated emission of a photon occurs when a photon of the same frequency hits an excited atom; that is, a photon stimulates the emission of an equal photon.

Furthermore, the stimulated photon has the same frequency as the incident photon and emerges in the same direction and phase.

The stimulated emission requires an incoming photon and an excited atom. The excited state's energy must be $\Delta E = hf$ above the ground state (h is Planck's constant, f-frequency, and E-energy).

Otherwise, the atom cannot make a quantum leap and emit a photon at the same frequency.

Now imagine that you have an extensive collection of atoms and that many of them are excited $\Delta E = hf$ above the earth state. Introducing a photon at frequency f can stimulate a quantum jump in one of the excited atoms to end up with two equal photons. Each of these two photons can then go on and stimulate two other identical photons, resulting in four "cloned" photons. If you have a vast population of excited atoms, you will have a large army of equal and cloned photons due to the waterfall effect.

This is precisely the "amplification" of the stimulated emission from which the laser derives its name.

Our description of amplification is based on having many excited atoms.

However, atoms prefer to be in their ground state. So, something needs to be done to prepare an extensive collection of excited-state atoms. This is called *population reversal,* and there are many ways to achieve it. However, it is necessary to have more atoms in the excited state than in the earth state in all cases. Otherwise, more photons will be absorbed than those emitted, and the waterfall will run out.

The process can be helped by placing a pair of mirrors on each end of the collection of atoms. One mirror should be 100% reflective, while the other should be partially transparent. This will allow a coherent, one-way beam of light to escape from one end and continue doing useful things. The first laser in the world consisted of a flash lamp coiled around a ruby rod inserted between a pair of mirrors. The flashing lamp generated a population reversal of atoms in the ruby crystal, and mirrors bounced photons back and forth to build a cascade of stimulated photons.

Today, lasers are available in all shapes and sizes.

The population of atoms, or "laser medium," is usually some form of gas or solid. Also, different lasers use different population inversion schemes. Lasers can also be set to emit light continuously or in pulses, and the pulse's energy and the pulse's duration can vary widely.

You meet lasers of many varieties every day.

For example, in the supermarket checkout lane, lasers are used to understand the price of the purchased items by scanning the laser beam through the bar code. The item's price is obtained by a detector that measures the laser light reflected by the barcode.

CD and DVD players scan the disc's surface, where small pits have been burned to digitally encode the images and music that we are trying to see and hear.

Lasers are also used by laser printers, which use them to transfer toner to printed pages.

Lasers have also revolutionized medicine.

Small pulsed lasers are used in surgery because they can emit energy in a very precise way and in tiny places, thus preventing unnecessary damage to nearby organs and tissues. They are also handy and minimally invasive in eye surgery, including retinal reattachment and vision correction.

The GPS

Maybe you have already heard of the Global Positioning System—or indeed its acronym, GPS—since most probably you have a navigator or cell phone.

Nevertheless, do you know that GPS would never have been born except for the laws of quantum physics? This is because, on every GPS satellite, there is an atomic clock.

From alarm clocks to Swatch wristwatches, almost every watch counts time by recording something that occurs at a specific regular frequency.

The pendulum of a pendulum clock, for example, swings back and forth about once per second (or a frequency of one hertz), so about 60 of these equals one minute.

A modern wristwatch is based on a quartz crystal, which oscillates more than 10,000 times per second. It takes many more cycles to count one minute, but the principle is the same.

We can also measure the frequency using a quantum jump in a given atom—not the speed with which quantum jumps occur, which can be random, but the frequency carried by the photons emitted when they do.

Since this frequency is given by the difference in atomic energy levels, which is the same for each atom of the same type, it is possible to use a collection of similar atoms to maintain time.

In theory, all it takes to create an atomic clock is to know the transition frequency of your particular atom. So, you can simply sit down and figure out how many swings equals one second.

In practice, you must also make sure that your atoms are in a very stable environment so there are no involuntary changes in their energy levels.

You can make a clock that lacks a second only once every 50 million years if you can do that!

Since the energy of each photon is very low, real-world atomic clocks need some form of amplification.

Therefore, the first atomic clocks were based on the stimulated emission in the microwave range—the so-called masers.

Usually, atomic clocks use a higher power oscillator (like a quartz crystal), which is "locked" to the atomic transition frequency with an electronic feedback mechanism.

GPS itself is based on a network of satellites, each of which travels in a circular orbit approximately 20,000 kilometers above the earth's surface. Each contains an atomic clock at the same frequency, that is, the time kept on one satellite is the time kept on another (within about one-billionth of a second). Besides, each satellite continuously transmits its position and time. The classical physics of Isaac Newton defines the position.

Meanwhile, on Earth, your GPS receiver can detect the transmission signals of at least four satellites at all times, wherever you go. The receiver then defines its position by calculating its distance from these four satellites.

This can be done because the transmitted signals travel towards the receiver at the speed of light (c) and therefore cover the distance (r) between the satellite and the receiver in a time $\Delta t = r/c$. The receiver measures the discrepancy between its time and that of the satellite, then calculates the distance as $r = c$

$\times \Delta t$. This informs the receiver that it is located on a sphere of radius r centered on the satellite's known position.

When the other three satellites are considered, the receiver determines that it is located on four spheres of known rays and centers. Two of these spheres intersect in a circle, while the third sphere intersects this circle in two points. The fourth sphere determines the position unequivocally.

All this is based on the GPS receiver, which measures time very accurately.

So, does our smartphone need its atomic clock? Fortunately, no. The GPS receiver obtains its time from the four satellites by calculating the three positions of the coordinates (x, y, z) and the time. Solving four unknown quantities with four equations is an easy task for even the most basic computer chip.

If you want to know your precise position, say less than 1 meter, you will need something more than quantum physics. You will need to add the theory of relativity. Since the satellites themselves are orbiting at such high speeds, their atomic clocks run faster than Earth's clocks. If your receiver does not correct this, it will cause errors in the positions of a few hundred meters.

The Anti-Gravity Wheel

Suppose you have a 19 kg wheel attached at the end of a meter-long shaft. You could attempt to lift and hold that shaft with one hand and keep it horizontal. You could try to do it for fun, but I can guarantee that you won't be able to do it unless you are a world-class body-builder. If, however, you could manage to rotate the wheel on the shaft at a few thousand rpm (with the help of a drill, for example), you would then be able to raise it with one hand and hold it, even above your head, with minimum effort. The wheel would seem light as a feather.

How is this possible? This is due to the gyroscopic precession.

Instead of pulling the wheel down to the ground as one might expect, the weight of the object creates torque that pushes it around, and therefore the wheel feels light when it turns. It can be seen that the pair vector increases the angular momentum in the same direction as the couple. If there is no angular momentum at the beginning, the new momentum oscillates in the direction of the couple. If there was an angular momentum at the beginning, the direction would change in the direction of the angular momentum, causing the precession.

CHAPTER 12: HOW QUANTUM PHYSICS CAN HELP US FIGHT CLIMATE CHANGE

As humans, we are inherently limited to what we can observe through the five senses. Quantum physics, however, tells us that everything is made up of particles called *quanta*. These quanta are not limited by the same constraints as our five senses; they could potentially exist in two places at once or take any form. It's up to our minds to choose one reality and stick with it.

Quantum physicists have provided possible explanations for how quantum theory could be applied elsewhere in order to help combat climate change. For example, some companies are using this knowledge to develop greener technology or even to engineer cheaper ways of storing solar energy for future use.

As a physicist, you can use your knowledge to look at other science areas that could benefit from the application of quantum theory. These areas may include climate change, the oil industry, or even how to make money in the stock market.

Here are ways quantum physics can help us fight climate change:

Quantum Vibrations May Change Ocean Water into Clouds

Scientific American has described how some scientists think that quantum physics may be responsible for the creation of clouds. The particles that make up water molecules are very small; they can act like waves on the ocean, which sometimes results in foggy skies.

The theory is called *quantum condensation*. At low temperatures, water molecules can become very excited, and this energy vibration (a "briefly excited state") can also vibrate clouds. This has been observed on Earth; for example, during cloud development near cold nights on the ground or in the upper atmosphere.

Quantum physics may also help us fight climate change by creating clouds that block the sun and turn into precipitation.

Quantum Mechanics Can Store Solar Energy

Quantum storage would be handy for such things as solar panels, wind power generators (turbines), and nuclear energy reactors. Quantum mechanics could make energy storage cost-effective and efficient.

One proposed method is to use two types of cold atoms: atoms with an electric charge (called ions) and neutral atoms (atoms that aren't charged). By combining this technique with other elements, we could store solar energy in a battery for later use during times without sunlight.

Under normal conditions, energy cannot be stored for long periods of time. However, using cool atoms and lasers, we can store solar energy for a long period of time. This could be used as a supplement to solar power and even provide substitute power during times of night and cold weather.

Other methods for implementing the use of quantum mechanics to store solar energy include the following:

• Sunlight activates quantum switches that either turn on current or turn off current (similar to how your computer uses binary code).

• Using sunlight, water could turn into oxygen and hydrogen, which are then stored as fuel. When you need more electricity, the process is reversed.

Using Quantum Entanglement Could Provide Clean Energy

There are many possible ways to utilize entanglement with quantum mechanics to produce clean energy. Entanglement is where two particles share the same existence, even though a great distance separates them.

One of the most commercially viable ways of using entanglement is through quantum computing, but this isn't how we can fight climate change.

Instead, one method of using quantum mechanics for producing clean energy is through fusion reactors. These devices use high-temperature plasmas to create nuclear fusion, which releases tremendous amounts of energy without creating any pollution or radiation waste.

Currently, these reactors are very tricky to build because of how hot they get, but using entanglement may help create an easier process. For example, two lasers are used to manipulate the plasma until it reaches the correct state.

Quantum Mechanics May Help Us Store Gas for Long Periods of Time

Gas storage is especially useful in vehicles with internal combustion engines because it can help with air pollution. We can store natural gas for decades without losing any energy or harming the environment.

Another quantum technology that's being developed is hydrogen fuel cell vehicles, which utilize electricity from hydrogen gas-powered catalysts. These catalysts can convert hydrogen into electricity, but this requires a slow and steady supply of gas. At the same time, these cars will also reduce air pollution because they don't need air filters or other ways to remove harmful toxins.

Quantum Mechanics Could Be Used to Manage Renewable Resources Better

By learning how quantum mechanics can help us manage renewable resources, we could better use natural resources when they're not being utilized or when their use is inefficient. This could be used to make more efficient solar panels, wind turbines, and even hydrogen fuel cells for vehicles since it gives them a longer lifespan.

Quantum Mechanics Can Sacrifice Particles to Clean the Atmosphere

One of the most popular ways of reducing carbon dioxide levels is to burn things that are rich in carbon. This means that the plant has already captured energy from sunlight, which is then used to create sugar or other biomass materials. But burning these plants creates more CO2, which oxidizes and turns into pollution.

The idea of "clean coal" comes from quantum physics because this theory can help us destroy pollutants without creating any waste matter or byproducts. There are two main ideas for how this can be done:

- Ionization is where some particles' electrons are stripped off their atomic cores by ionizing radiation (gamma rays). Then, as the ionized particles travel into a container, they turn back into their normal states.

- Electromagnetic radiation is where electrons are stripped off of atoms by bombardment with gamma rays. This produces plasma particles that change the particle's spin so they either stay in their normal spin states or are in a state of spin-flip called *spinor* states.

The carbon emission process can be stabilized by placing the radioactive source close to the plant while adding energy to create electric energy from gamma rays emitted by the radioactive material.

This type of process produces no waste products and doesn't produce any pollution that's harmful to humans or animals. However, it's not fully developed yet.

Quantum Mechanics Can Be Used to Create Biological Noise

This method uses the natural chaos of quantum mechanics to create noise in cells, which changes their DNA and creates unique patterns that make each cell special. This technology could also be used to vaccinate cells without the need for vaccinations or other harmful chemicals or treatments.

Quantum Mechanics Can Help Us Make Long-Distance Power Transmission More Efficient

One of the biggest challenges when it comes to transmitting power across a long distance is getting rid of wasted energy due to resistance in a wire's circuit and interference from surrounding objects. We can overcome this challenge by using quantum computing with superconducting circuits.

CHAPTER 13: QUANTUM COGNITION AND CONSCIOUSNESS

Why Is Quantum So Mysterious?

One of the main explanations of why quantum physics is enigmatic is that it tends to be expressed or represented in terms of probability. Certainty seems the standard in our everyday macro culture. Either the cat is living, or it's gone. In all explanations of quantum phenomenon, remember that objects are unknown and therefore only likely to an observer, or whether anyone is attempting to quantify something. The key factor is the observer. An observer with probabilities defines quantum physics. Probability is just a type of mathematics, and mathematics is an invention or abstract notion that resides in the mind. You calculate or observe stuff and mentally allocate probabilities to what you are testing or calculating. For little else, they are labeled 'error lines.' There are limitations on how you can detect or quantify stuff correctly, and that's because the very process of observing or measuring influences what you are examining or calculating. So far, so good. But, what happens if you eliminate the spectator from the image (and the mental definition of probability)? After the Big Bang, no life, thought, and observer remained. If there were no observers around to allocate odds, should you always claim the microdomain was probabilistic? Human beings do not know precisely where the damn electron is, but they know Mother Nature! In reality, the electron 'knows' as well, more often than not, but we will not go on that in this book.

Quantum Mechanics and the Brain

Quantum mechanics is the study of how small particles and subatomic particles interact with one another. Quantum mechanics has given way to radio, television, radar, and even today's electronics technology. Perhaps most importantly for our understanding of the brain, it has also been applied to neurological phenomena. The study of quantum mechanics can provide significant insights into brain function by attending to its implications in homeostasis and consciousness.

Despite what some may say about its perplexing counter-intuitive nature, quantum mechanics is now one of the most accepted theories in modern physics. Quantum mechanical effects are so ubiquitous that it would be difficult to find a place where they are not present. For example, when a plant turns toward the sun, or an animal turns towards food, they exhibit quantum effects.

The key to understanding quantum mechanics is that we cannot make assumptions based on our everyday experiences. An everyday experience can only approximate certain phenomena due to the size and time scale involved in those experiences. A person standing on top of a building may think the ground below them will support them up until they fall through it. In reality, if you attempted to walk to the center of a building, you would fall through. We make similar mistakes when we try to explain quantum effects. This can be seen when people think that the wave function collapsing is the same as a particle "choosing" a direction or location. A key point is that we cannot look at everyday experiences and assume they hold in any scientific model.

It may seem like I'm going off on a tangent here, but this is an important point for neuroscience because it is so easy to get confused about what consciousness relates to in the brain. It's not light bulbs switching on or off; it's not genes or neurons firing; or chemistry within synapses. These are all products of consciousness and can't be equated with it. These "smaller" things are the building blocks that make up the brain, but consciousness is their end-product not their source. That end product is the "self", or the ego.

We can see this at play with some theories of quantum mechanics, especially Everett's Many Worlds interpretation. This theory makes some assumptions about both time and consciousness being non-linear which has significant implications for how we view our own conscious experience about time. On the surface it would seem that this theory is highly counter-intuitive. However, the core idea, albeit hypothetical, is quite simple.

This theory begins with the assumption that many worlds are existing at once, but rather than thinking about them as separate from one another (like a possible and actual world), we can think about them as existing within a single world with different "characters". The quantum observer in each world then experiences a single reality described by the probability wave function and from their perspective, which only exists at that point in time and space, they experience one version of their life. They can never communicate with other quantum observers because they do not experience overlapping realities. They are separate within their single experience because they exist at different times and different places.

When we think about consciousness being non-linear and consistent with the Copenhagen interpretation of quantum mechanics, we assume that when we get more educated and experience more things, our understanding of the universe becomes more complete and we can apply that to our consciousness. This manifests in various ways as we mature from a child's mind to an adult's mind. We can observe this when someone is talking about quantum mechanics for the first time. They are often quite confused about even basic concepts such as the wave function or probability wave function of quantum mechanics. At first, the discussion appears paradoxical until the person is shown how it relates to everyday experiences. Similarly, it's easy to think that consciousness doesn't really exist until we start experiencing things. In both of these cases, however, the mind reaches a point where it can make generalizations about the universe and apply them to itself.

This type of development is what we would expect when we try to explain how consciousness relates to general neuroscience research on the brain. The idea is that over time and with each passing experience, our nervous system is better able to understand itself by observing its own behavior. If you want to predict something about your future brain state or behavioral experience, you should look at what you have done in the past and use this understanding as a guide for future neuronal activity.

A Consciousness Model

Based on the research that I've seen, here is a best-guess model of how consciousness relates to general neuroscience research on the brain. I'm not saying that this is how it actually is, and it could very well be wrong given what we know today. But if this model were true, then there should be some indications of it within neuroscience itself or at least theoretical results that are consistent with this interpretation. The model assumes both non-linearity and locality, so many of these findings will not make sense unless you do some background reading about these principles in quantum mechanics and general relativity if you are unfamiliar with them.

If this model is true, then there should be indications that consciousness is non-local and not directly caused by physical processes. Non-locality would mean that consciousness can exist without being directly caused by a physical process or locality would mean that the location of consciousness within the brain is not fixed. There are two major ways to interpret these results: first, they can be thought of as purely products of our mind and second, they can be seen as a property of reality itself. The first view leads us to believe that we are all living in a simulation, but I think this is overly narrow and doesn't take into account the more important connection between our minds and the universe as a whole. The second view leads us to believe that consciousness is a fundamental property of the universe with which we are all connected. In this model I'm going to assume that non-locality is a fundamental property of the universe and see how well it fits the neuroscience research.

"Consciousness can exist without being directly caused by a physical process."

Non-locality. One big issue with modern neuroscience and consciousness research is that we don't know where consciousness resides in the brain. For example, if one part of your brain dies, does that mean you're gone as well? Well, no one knows for sure but there are implications in science that suggest you are still around despite losing important parts of your brain. One good example of this is in split-brain patients where the corpus callosum, the pathway between the left and right hemispheres of the brain, is severed. Researchers found that the left hemisphere and right hemisphere have different personalities. The left hemisphere will be logical and conscious whereas the right hemisphere will be emotional, subconscious and reactionary. The difficulty for neuroscience comes here when we realize that split-brain patients aren't actually two separate people. They act as two distinct personalities but they are both controlled by one mind. This is impossible according to modern neuroscience so it naturally raises some questions about how consciousness works in relation to physical processes in our brain.

Researchers have proposed that the left and right hemispheres of the brain are similar to two distinct computers (the left hemisphere as the conscious, logical part and the right hemisphere as the subconscious, emotional part). Yet if this were true, then we would expect that they would share some information. Yet in split-brain patients it was found that they can't share information between their hemispheres. If this is true then it directly contradicts our current understanding of how reality works. If two computers are connected by a network and cannot communicate with each other, then there is a problem with our reality because we can clearly communicate between two computer-like things within our mind: our two hemispheres.

My proposed solution to this conundrum is that the information transfer between the left and right "computers" (as a model of the left and right hemispheres) is non-local. This makes complete sense if you think about it because a computer is made of electronic components, which are made from physical atoms, whereas our mind seems to be made up of something else, some kind of non-physical information. This provides an interesting explanation as to why we cannot communicate with one another even though we are able to talk with one another.

The connection isn't physical but it also isn't mental because we can't physically see-through walls or minds via psychic powers either. Another way to think of this is that there are many waves in our universe, one for each person in the world, and they can all interact with one another but they don't do so locally.

My theory is that this non-locality in the brain and all over the universe is a fundamental property of reality itself. This means that it's not just happening within our brain but it's also happening outside of us as well in between people. This would explain why my consciousness can talk with another consciousness, we're just two universal waves talking to each other, two distinct parts of the same whole. To help understand how this could work, I can use an analogy to describe how this could work at a quantum level.

This would imply that we're all connected as part of one big organism (the universe), which causes us to feel like we are separate even though we are not. We would be able to feel emotions, have thoughts, and experience the world in completely different ways without actually being physically separate beings. This would also explain why we can't communicate with each other because our vibrations (or information) don't nestle together like people do at night. It doesn't nestle together because they are travelling at different speeds that prevent communication rather than it being local and on top of that, reality is non-local.

My theory also explains why certain people can experience "out of body experiences." These happen when the vibrations or information between two minds is so great that it creates a new self. We know this happens with certain drugs but we don't know why it happens. It's also possible that these experiences are a physical effect of the information travelling between the two minds. So, if our mind is a collective entity and we are all part of one whole, then it would make sense that when two minds are very close to one another then we can experience this "out of body experience." I have no proof for this theory, but I think it is more plausible than what modern neuroscience has to say about consciousness.

"The brain is aware of its environment. Certain stimuli (such as light hitting the retina, or a thought of hitting your fingers with a hammer) may cause the brain to send out electrical impulses (action potentials)."

Non-locality. This could be very similar to what I said above and it could potentially explain consciousness itself. If our mind is one entity then it would be non-local and if this one entity expands outwards then all the information in it would remain non-local too. The only problem with this theory is that there is no way that my mind can expand outwards into someone else's mind because there is no material connection between us (as far as we know).

Consciousness and nonlinear quantum evolution

It can be seen that the distinguishability of nonorthogonal states violates the superposition principle, and thus consciousness introduces one kind of nonlinear quantum evolution by such distinguishability. This kind of nonlinearity is definite, not stochastic. This immediately raises two questions. The first one is how consciousness can solve the difficulties of nonlinear quantum mechanics. The second question is much deeper: why does consciousness introduce the nonlinear quantum evolution? In the following, we will briefly answer these two questions.

It is well known that nonlinear quantum mechanics has a general characteristic: The description of composite systems depends on a particular basis in a Hilbert space. This is a severe difficulty for nonlinear quantum mechanics, indeed, as it makes such theories inconsistent. However, as we have demonstrated above, the consciousness of an observer will naturally select a privileged basis in its state space; a conscious observer can be aware of his definite perceptions, but not the superpositions of such perceptions. Thus, the nonlinear quantum evolution introduced by consciousness is logically consistent and may exist. On the other hand, as noted before, nonlinear quantum mechanics permits the existence of FTL communication. This is also consistent with the suggested mechanism for FTL communication.

Now we turn to the second question. Why does consciousness have the superpower to violate the quantum superposition principle? As noted before, a conscious observer can be aware of the change of its perception state, especially the transition from a superposition of different conscious perceptions to one of the conscious perceptions. But a physical measuring device, which is assumed to have no consciousness, cannot record this transition according to quantum mechanics (if the theory is nonlinear, then the device can), though it can indeed record some other changes of its physical state, such as its temperature change, etc. BUT why is consciousness special? The reason is that the physical state is indefinite for a superposition of different perceptions, while the conscious awareness is always definite, no matter what it is[42]. The particular link between physical states and consciousness introduces the definite nonlinearity in the quantum evolution of the physical state of a conscious observer.

For example, when the physical state of a conscious observer is $\psi 1 + \psi 2$, its conscious state is x12, and the total state is not $\psi 1 x1 + \psi 2 x2$, but $(\psi 1 + \psi 2)$ x12. Moreover, since this conscious perception can be put into memory and further lead to some external outputs by verbal report or physical action, the last physical state will be $(\psi 1 + \psi 2)$ $\psi 12$. This introduces one kind of (definite) nonlinearity for the quantum evolution of the physical states.

The above argument can be summarized in a clearer way. A conscious mental state, unlike a physical state, cannot be an indefinite superposition state. We either have conscious perception x or have no conscious perception x. We cannot both have conscious perception x and have no conscious perception x. We know this by self-awareness. In short, consciousness rejects quantum superposition and thus violates the superposition principle.

CHAPTER 14: EINSTEIN'S CONTRIBUTIONS TO QUANTUM PHYSICS

After a moment of reflection, Einstein discovered what he describes as his happiest moment: when a man falls freely, he will not feel his weight. In 1907, only two years after he developed his theory of relativity, the vision appeared to him, and this he described as the essential basis of the theory of general relativity. As simple as the idea was, it took him about 10 years to properly elaborate.

Newtonian mechanics made provisions that we are all under the influence of the earth's gravitational field, and this tends to pull us down. According to Einstein, he said that there is a freedom that is experienced by free fall, and this is what individuals who engage in free fall carry out as hobbies. Astronauts in space also experience this feeling in the form of weightlessness because, in space, they are no longer under the influence of the attraction of Earth's gravitational force. The basis of the understanding of Einstein was that when a person jumps up, in that very brief moment of suspension and in essence, there was no difference in principle between a vessel in orbit around the earth and a ball which we throw here on Earth. In essence, both are in free fall; both are, for the duration of their motion, satellites of Earth.

The Equivalence Principle

With this new understanding of the world, which is different from what Newton had proposed, Einstein was able to formulate the equivalence principle, and the essence of this theory was that the gravitational field is equivalent to a field of acceleration. In order to obtain this principle, he drew upon a fundamental property of gravitational fields, which was already proposed by Galileo and which was included in the equations proposed by Newton. This was the theory that the acceleration communicated to a body by a gravitational field is independent of its mass.

Einstein saw the need to develop a general theory after defining his theory of special relativity for so many reasons. There was a need to fully make the laws of Newton fit into the law, just as how mechanics of free particles and electrodynamics did. The equations of Newton were totally invariant under the classical transformation of Galileo but didn't show this under Lorentz transformation. This created a division in the field of physics: it was split into two and contradicted with the principle of relativity, which necessitates the validity of the same fundamental laws in all situations.

The theory of relativity showed some contradictions with the presuppositions in the Newtonian theory. So, Einstein thought it was necessary to develop a relativist theory for gravitation as it was a logical necessity.

Another problem came up, and it was based on the fact that the relativist approach explicitly gives itself the problem of changes of reference systems and their influence on the form of physical laws; special relativity only provided a small part of the answers. The frames of references considered were in uniform translation, at constant speeds with respect to one another. However, the real world constantly shows us rotations and accelerations due to the multiple forces at work, such as gravity, or inversely, causing new forces like inertial force.

The general theory of relativity was introduced to provide answers to such questions as, what are the laws of transformation in the case of accelerated frames of reference? Why would such frames of reference not be as valid for writing the laws of physics as inertial frames of reference?

Einstein approached this problem by seeking out a theory that would address the relativist theory of gravitation and generalize relativity to non-inertial systems and carry this out in a single endeavor. This was possible due to the equivalence principle, which made it possible. In order to accomplish this, if the field of acceleration and the gravitational field are locally indistinguishable, the two problems of describing changes in the coordinates systems, including those that are accelerated and those subject to a gravitational field, come down to a single problem. Another problem encountered was that such an approach is not reducible to "making relativist" Newtonian gravitation. Einstein proposed to solve the problem of Newton's theory through general relativity, whereas other physicists sought to solve this problem through a simple reformulation: by bringing in a force that propagated at the speed of light. This was a new theory, a theory of framework (curved spacetime, now a dynamic variable) connected with its contents, and no longer only a theory of "objects" in a rigid preexisting framework seen in Newton's absolute space.

The Einstein's Elevator Experiment and the Strong Equivalence Principle

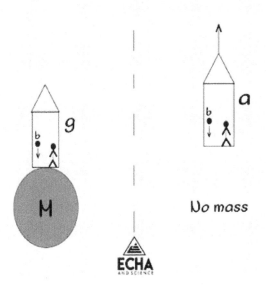

This was a necessary step because the special relativity itself was not enough to satisfy a very crucial point: the space-time which characterized it. Although it included in its description a space and a time which are no longer absolute when taken individually, it still remains absolute when it is taken as a four-dimensional "object." Although the works of Ernst Mach inspired him, Einstein had come to think that using an absolute space-time could have no physical meaning, but rather, that its geometry would have to be in correspondence with its material and energetic contents. After studying the inertial forces, Einstein adopted the opposite conclusion rather than the approach adopted by Newton, which caused him to introduce absolute space.

The Problem of Inertial Forces

The existence of inertial forces limits the theory of space-time, and this poses a problem also to the absolute and relative nature of motion. Einstein was able to draw a lot from the work of Mach regarding this area. Mach proposed that the relativity of motion did not apply solely to uniform motion in translation. Rather, all motion of whatever sort was by essence relative; this has been discovered by Poincare and also by Huygens.

Although these theories may seem a bit contradictory to facts. Galileo already observed that it was quite impossible to characterize the state of the inertial motion of a body in an absolute manner (only the speed of a body with respect to another has physical meaning); it proved to be different in the case of accelerated motions. Thus, when one considers a body turning about itself, the existence of its rotational motion seems to be able to be felt in a manner that is totally intrinsic to the body. There will be no need for another body of reference; it is just enough to verify whether or not a centrifugal force appears, which tends to deform the rotating body.

Taking into consideration the thought experiment of Galileo's ship, the difference between inertial movement and rotational motion becomes heightened. It was concluded that no kind of experiment can be conducted in the cabin of a ship traveling in uniform and rectilinear motion with respect to the earth is capable of determining the existence of the boat's movement: Galileo said that "motion is like nothing." In order to observe relative motion, you'll need to open up a hole and then watch the shore pass; only at that point can you actually observe relative motion. If par adventure, the boat increases its speed—acceleration—or turns about itself, then all the objects which are present in the cabin will be pushed towards the walls. This will enable the observer to notice movement without having to look outside. This shows that accelerated motion is totally definable by a purely local experiment.

This observation led Newton to assume that absolute space can be defined, whereas Leibniz and Mach were of the opinion that space would not have any meaning independent of the objects it contains.

Mach proposed a possible solution to this problem that was totally different from what was proposed by Newton. He began from the principle of relativity of all motion, at which he arrived at the natural conclusion that the turning body, within which had inertial forces, must turn not with respect to a certain absolute space but with respect to other material bodies. The bodies being referred to here are not closed bodies, as these bodies are exposed to fluctuations of distribution, and this would provoke visual fluctuations of inertial systems. This wasn't acceptable since it is quite easier to observe and verify the coherence of these systems over great distances. Thus, if we look, motionless concerning the earth, at the night sky, we do not see the stars turning. Nevertheless, if we turn about ourselves, we feel our arms spreading out due to inertial forces, and, in raising our eyes toward the sky, we can see it turn. Mach's initial proposal was that within the same frame of reference, the arms are raised and the sky turns, and this will be true for two points of the earth separated by thousands of kilometers. The suggestion made by Mach was that the common frame of reference is determined by the entirety of the distant matter, of bodies "at infinity," of which the cumulative gravitational influence would be at the origin of inertial forces. In simple words, Bach proposed that the body would turn with respect to a gram of reference, not absolute but universal. An absolute motion would be defined in itself, independently of all objects. However, Mach argued that all motion is relative, remaining defined with respect to an "object," even if this body is the universe in its entirety.

Einstein proposed a solution through his principle

of the equivalence principle and general relativity, and they both integrated some of these ideas yet still created a distinction from the principle of Mach, although he had similar premises. The distribution of matter and energy in the whole world of the universe determines the geometric structure of spacetime, and then the movements of bodies are brought about within the framework of this geometry tied to matter.

Relativity of Gravity

This was one of the great ideas proposed by Einstein in 1907. This theory was critical as it helped shape the understanding of the basic concept of gravity in a manner different from Newtonian mechanics. If an observer descends in free fall within a gravitational field, they no longer feel their weight, which means that they no longer feel the existence of this field itself. This idea at the onset was viewed with skepticism, but we have seen in movies and in PR television programs how astronauts float weightlessly in their ships and how objects leave them floating at a constant speed. This idea was revolutionary because it proved that gravity doesn't just exist on its own, and the existence of gravity is dependent on the choice of a frame of reference.

Adopting this proposition, he was able to create a distinction from the former idea of gravity. In the

Newtonian model, gravity was absolute. It has been recognized by Newton as universal; it was indeed a physical phenomenon of which the existence does not seem to depend on such a condition of observation.

However, when an enclosed area is allowed to fall freely under gravity, and then we put in motion a body at a certain velocity with respect to this area, the body will move in a straight line at a constant speed concerning the walls of the enclosure; a body initially immobile in respect to the wall will stay thus during the movement of the enclosure's fall. In other words, all experiments that we can perform there would confirm that we are in an initial frame of reference! This means that although gravity is universal, it can be canceled out solely by a judicious choice of the coordinate system. Einstein was able to understand that the understanding of gravity is dependent on the choice of a coordinate system.

CHAPTER 15: FUTURE OF QUANTUM PHYSICS

This has been a heck of a ride through the history of quantum physics, huh? We're going to finish strong with a glimpse of the state of quantum physics as we head into the future and maybe toss in one last mind-warping topic. If you guessed string theory, you'd be correct! Let's ease into that, though—we'll start with something a little lighter and walk-through quantum physics in action in the things that we use every day. Then we'll attack string theory. It'll be fun!

Everyday Objects Doing Extraordinary Things

In your pocket, right now, you hold the key to all human knowledge. It's your cell phone, and it runs on quantum physics. No, really. There are a couple of different applications of quantum mechanics and quantum chemistry going on inside your tiny personal computer, communication device, and positioning beacon. Oh, you've never thought about your phone in quite that way? It certainly makes a difference in how you consider this fantastic little machine.

First, let's take into account the computer chip itself. It is a marvel of quantum technology. Most chips are made from silicon, an abundant element with some unique characteristics. When silicon is layered up in a certain way, its electrons start to create a band structure. Simply put, the electron waves harmonize, and the silicon becomes able to conduct electromagnetic waves in a predictable pattern. Using band structure patterns is something quantum physicists rely on to give them feedback about how the atoms within a material are behaving because it is an observable phenomenon. It gives them the ability to determine whether a material will be a good conductor. Silicon fits the bill, and along with technological advancements, this has lent the ability to build smaller and smaller computer chips and to shrink the size of computing machines from taking up whole buildings to fitting in our jeans pockets.

Your cell phone is also capable of sending and receiving data across a cellular network. What does that mean exactly? These networks rely on radio signals to allow people to send and receive calls, text messages, emails, and other communications right on your phone, anywhere there is cellular coverage. Cell towers are now in 95% of the world's inhabitable spaces, some of them "hiding" as trees, and they use radio waves of varying frequencies to relay data to one another, finally reaching your device, which is encoded with your personal frequency attached to your phone number. Pretty cool, huh? It's even more remarkable when you consider that the technology has become so advanced that the giant bag phones of the 1980s have become a novelty item and museum dust collectors in less than four decades.

Cellular towers use different frequencies to avoid jamming their own signals, and they operate at varying wavelengths depending on the area in which they are built. Rural towers use lower frequencies with longer wavelengths to cast their net to a larger area, and urban towers use higher wavelengths and frequencies to penetrate the maze of buildings and concrete. This also leads to the need for more towers and cells in urban areas because the high-frequency waves can't travel very far. As many cellular providers upgrade their equipment to ultrafast next-generation equipment, they are also shrinking the size of the cellular transmitters to fit into urban spaces and onto utility poles. This allows them to put more cells into smaller places and not look as obvious as the old "tree" towers, which are ridiculous, anyway. Cell signals rely on "line of sight" to be able to communicate with each other, and those towers always end up being way taller than the forest around them. But they tried.

Another fantastic thing your cell phone can do is tap into global positioning satellites, and that's all thanks to quantum physics, too. GPS capabilities are built into most computer-driven devices these days, which is why your computer at home can show you which stores are nearby, and you can look at detailed maps of your neighborhood and pretty much anywhere on earth. GPS uses triangulation to determine your location, which is relayed from your device to satellites orbiting the earth to find the location where you wish to go. If that isn't sciencey enough, the mechanism behind this action is really dependent on quantum physics.

Every time a signal is picked up by a positioning satellite, the computer within the satellite begins performing a series of rapid calculations to convert your location from a coordinate into a length of time. Using the calculations of several satellites at once, the system can determine your location within a small radius and tell you how long it will take for you to get from Point A to Point B, which it has also calculated within a few hundred feet. Global positioning satellites depend on atomic clocks to calculate this timing, and those clocks are run by tiny nuclear engines powered by atoms whose exact decay takes one second to release an electron. So, the next time you're heading to an unfamiliar place and take your phone out of your pocket to get directions and travel times, think about all the marvelous machinery, driven by quantum physics, that is performing what seems like a simple task.

Got the World on a String

Okay, deep breath—let's tackle string theory. As we know, physicists have spent entire careers trying to develop a unified field theory, and it is always gravity that doesn't cooperate. Having one giant, provable body of scientific work that explains everything in the universe would be awfully convenient, wouldn't it? Except that for all the fundamental forces of physics, we have yet to be able to observe gravity on its particle level—gravitons are still an object of mere speculation. We know that wave-particle duality is a genuine, observable phenomenon, and that gives us the basis for string theory.

String theory was first introduced in the 1970s as a potential candidate for the theory of everything. It puts forth the hypothesis that perhaps particles aren't moving independently of each other but are instead the ends of invisible cosmic strings. Some particles may mark the end of openended strings (a particle at each end), and some may be the closing point where the two ends attach in a singularity. String theorists— and remember this is a significantly simplified explanation—believe that the open strings represent the strong, weak, and electromagnetic forces of nature, and the closed strings represent gravitational forces. Studying how these strings interact would be possible to trace the source of gravity and eventually find its particles. Right?

Sort of. String theory didn't initially account for the strings coming apart and joining together in different places in space-time, and so they wanted to put them on a plane to control them. Putting them on a plane meant limiting the strings to set dimensions, and limiting the strings to set dimensions meant that string theory could no longer be used to hypothesize about controlling the fundamental forces to achieve accelerated passage through space-time. So, the next thing that string theorists did was toss in a "whatever" clause. They said that maybe there are up to three new dimensions we just haven't been able to discover yet.

String theory might seem far-fetched, and it's far from having been proven, but it does have its roots in some of the most substantial quantum physics contributions, so it shouldn't be thrown out just yet. String theory, like any other unified field theory, wants to marry relativity (dealing with the largest cosmic objects) and quantum theory (dealing with the tiniest objects) into one theory of quantum gravity. By alleging that each particle is actually one end of a cosmic string, and thinking about Bohr's theory of complementarity, then both ends of the string should balance themselves out. Some theorize that there is a fermion on one end and a boson on the other, and when they meet in a closed loop, the resulting collision releases energy and a graviton. If that could be proven to be accurate, then string theory might really have something going for it, but until then, we're stuck not being able to harness the power of gravity for our benefit.

One of the biggest proponents of string theory is physicist Edward Witten, a mathematical and theoretical physicist at Einstein's old stomping ground, the Institute for Advanced Study at Princeton. Witten is the developer of the M-theory version of string theory, and he has long proposed to solve the problem once and for all with math. Except in all his years of working on it, the math hasn't added up. The amount of energy needed to produce a graviton doesn't match the amount of energy of the particles entering the collision. Mass-equivalency tells us that something is off with those calculations, and no one is quite sure how to fix it.

The exciting thing about string theory, and the one that keeps people from giving up and looking elsewhere for the theory of everything, is the potential for exploring untapped dimensions. If just by attaching one end of a cosmic string to a different particle, we could change the very fabric of space-time and allow entrance into another dimension, then why wouldn't we be excited about string theory? That's an incredible, almost unimaginable possibility. String theory gives us a new way to think about how all matter is connected in a great cosmic dance.

String theory has its many detractors, and one person who never really bought into it was Stephen Hawking, perhaps the brightest mind in theoretical physics since Einstein himself. It may be that Hawking really thought string theory was bunk, or he was concerned with pushing his own theory of everything, but Hawking was sure that string theory was a long way from being proven. Hawking was also concerned with finding a resolution to the dilemma of gravity, but he centered his work on exploring black holes, not necessarily as wormholes between known areas of space-time, but as living, breathing portals into unknown dimensions. Despite his groundbreaking work on black hole radiation, gravitational fields, and the black hole information paradox (does physical data also get lost in the gravity of a black hole?), Hawking himself was never able to reconcile a unified field theory.

Perhaps there is no theory of everything, and these great scientific minds are simply chasing something that doesn't exist. One thing is for sure, though: they aren't going to stop looking. If a theory could be developed and proven that joins together quantum theory and relativity in a working, observable model of universal truth, that scientist or research team would go down in history as having a brilliance surpassing all the minds that came before. And, you also get a bunch of money when you win the Nobel Prize, so that's pretty cool.

CONCLUSION

Use this as a reference guide, incorporate it into your daily routine, and it's sure to improve your life. Read it everywhere and let every word make you feel excited and optimistic as you go about your activities.

It might be difficult at times, as physics is always associated with mathematics (which doesn't make physics any more attractive). Unfortunately, one cannot avoid math, which is indispensable for physics. Galileo Galilei (1564–1642), the father of modern physics, put it this way: The Book of Nature is written in the language of mathematics. Practically nothing can be explained without it.

The age-old question is whether mathematics is an invention of man or whether it has an independent existence. This is still controversial today, but most mathematicians and nearly all physicists tend to consider its independent existence. This idea goes back to Plato (428–348 BC). However, he did not speak of mathematics but of the world of ideas and perfect forms.

Which serves the universe best as a model? Let us join the majority and assume the independent existence of mathematics. So, what is the universe? By definition, it represents the totality of what exists. Consequently, it encompasses two worlds. One is the material world: the world of matter and energy, embedded in space and time. The universe also includes the world of mathematics, to which we ascribe an independent existence, detached from us humans.

But does the material world exist only as we know it? Undoubtedly no, because what we know is constructed by our brains. This applies both to the material world and to the world of mathematics. Both are different in reality, but there is undoubtedly a connection, and its nature is always somewhat hidden from us.

Therefore, physicists and mathematicians go the pragmatic route and ignore the fundamentally unknown differences. But I think one should always keep in mind that what we call the material world and the world of mathematics are "colored" by the human brain. We only know the human versions of these worlds. Aliens, if they exist, could therefore have a completely different idea of both worlds.

The mathematical physicist Roger Penrose (born in 1931) assumes the existence of three worlds. For him, there is also the world of consciousness. Undoubtedly, the material world is connected to it, for consciousness appears in the brain. But how is it generated? Neuroscientists have discovered that there are so-called correlates of consciousness in the brain. This means that a connection can be established between the occurrence of consciousness and the activity of the brain. But where does what we experience through our consciousness come from?

For example, the red of a sunset. Neuroscientists have nothing to say about this. They are increasingly able to decipher the structure and function of the brain using ever better investigation methods, but they do not come closer to explaining consciousness itself.

Obviously, there is an insurmountable and profound gap between it and what can be uncovered by the methods of natural science. This clearly shows that the current scientific view of the world is incomplete. But how should it be supplemented? I present a proposal that would provide the key to consciousness.

There are great differences in people's mathematical abilities, and where they come from is unclear. But what is certain is that mathematics is a gift, something that many are born with, because you can only learn it to a very limited extent. This is shown by the best mathematicians, such as Carl Friedrich Gauss (1777–1855) or Bernhard Riemann (1826–1866), who performed mathematical miracles as children without much training or knowledge. Even more impressive was the Indian Srinivasa Ramanujan (1887–1920). He had no formal education at all, but nevertheless, mathematical insights flowed effortlessly out of him.

As Paul Davies aptly says, "Some people can jump two meters high, but most can barely jump a meter. With the mathematical geniuses, it's as if a few could jump twenty meters high."

Why do we have access to the world of mathematics? That's a mystery because it doesn't bring any survival advantage. Then why did mathematical skills develop? Nobody knows.

People have always searched for what "holds the world together at its core" (Goethe, Faust). Yet, in fact, they have only found what they were looking for with quantum theory. It represents the most fundamental theory of physics, and all experiments carried out so far have confirmed its correctness. More precisely, they have confirmed its mathematical formalism. The problem is that its interpretation is still controversial. But this is exactly what makes the quantum theory so captivating.

It also provides what is probably the most mysterious phenomenon of all, which is entanglement. This has not received much public attention so far. Two intertwined objects can influence each other very quickly, even if they are many light-years apart. That's experimentally proven, and physicists are firmly convinced that there is no spatial limit. So far, entanglement has eluded any explanation. But it strongly suggests that behind the world perceived by our senses, there must also exist a world hidden from them.

Another inexplicable phenomenon is our consciousness. At first glance, there seems to be no connection between it and entanglement. But is that really true?

Indeed, the connection between the inner world and the inner nature of matter is very plausible due to the need for a solution to the mystery of entanglement and the explanation of consciousness. But there's no direct verification of it. Could this be possible someday?

An evident approach is the formation process of atoms and molecules because then the gate to the inner world opens, and information flows out of it, which causes the organization of the spatial relationships within the forming atom or molecule. This may become experimentally accessible someday, which would lead to direct evidence of both the inner world and the inner nature of matter.

But there's a problem: I'm an outsider. Therefore, my hypothesis of the inner world has not received any scientific attention so far, and this is necessary for its further development and, in particular, for the possible experiments just mentioned.

Principles of quantum theory can be applied to anything that has a nature. They can be applied to anti-quark expressions, solar anti-mass, infirm grandmothers, and children who shout too much, while c squared will allow for many conducive theories still to be put forward.

Yet, never let it be said that time doesn't have some kind of influence in the hereafter, and if my calculations are correct, this may be so; therefore, relativity theory may be a better option, and this may eventually be the case.

There is a world of sheer fascination out there—a world of underwater creatures we have no name for, of microscopic living beings that have survived every single catastrophe on Earth, of stars that have died out thousands of years ago and yet still continue to beam their light on us.

Mankind has grown a lot. From the very first spark of fire to the fast-moving internet connections that have brought billions of people together in a cyber-home that we are still learning to understand and play with, we have walked a path of thousands and thousands of years.

What might be shocking to some of you, dear readers, is that this is just the beginning of it all. If we were to compare the evolution of mankind so far to the development of a child, we would still be in our very early infancy.

We see the world around us, and we perceive it with all our senses. We have learned to cook as a sign of communication and intelligence. We have learned to reach out with our hands for food and information.

And yet, we still have a very long way to go. We still have to learn how to walk and talk, how to reach the stars, and how to embrace the beauty of everything around us beyond the limitations of our own cradle.

We owe our evolution to a large number of pretty amazing people from a very wide range of fields of knowledge: artists and writers who knew how to transgress meaning and create a language that moves past borders, nations, and traditions to encompass human emotion in all its glory. Scientists who knew how to ask the right questions and how to give answers that were never finite but always left room for more knowledge to be acquired.

The men and women who shaped this world are, without a doubt, an exceptional bunch. They are more than just thinkers and doers—they are shapers of the world in which we have all learned to live.

More than anything, though, they were visionaries who knew there was something more to what they did, who knew that self-sufficiency would lead us nowhere, but that childlike curiosity and experimentation would lead us everywhere.

Literature, music, arts, physics, chemistry, mathematics, history, geography, geology, computing—the garden of human knowledge has grown to be more than impressive. And in this vast garden, a tree has sprouted with big promises for the future: quantum physics

Get to the innate level that you were meant to reach, and don't hesitate to congratulate yourself when you finally obtain intuitive knowledge.

Made in the USA
Coppell, TX
06 August 2022